HE'S STILL HERE

HERE

THE BIOGRAPHY OF

JOAQUIN PHOENIX

HE'S STILL HERE

THE BIOGRAPHY OF

JOAQUIN PHOENIX

MARTIN HOWDEN

JOHN BLAKE

Published by John Blake Publishing Ltd,
3 Bramber Court, 2 Bramber Road,
London W14 9PB, England

www.johnblakepublishing.co.uk

First published in paperback in 2011

ISBN: 978 1 84358 340 0

British Library Cataloguing-in-Publication Data:

A catalogue record for this book is available
from the British Library.

Design by www.envydesign.co.uk

Printed in Great Britain by CPI Bookmarque, Croydon, CR0 4TD

1 3 5 7 9 10 8 6 4 2

Papers used by John Blake Publishing are natural, recyclable products
made from wood grown in sustainable forests. The manufacturing
processes conform to the environmental regulations of the
country of origin.

Every attempt has been made to contact the relevant
copyright-holders, but some were unobtainable. We would
be grateful if the appropriate people could contact us.

CONTENTS

CHAPTER ONE

WHAT'S IN A NAME?

In conversation, interviews and in life, he has had to deal with a multitude of queries about his name. How do you pronounce your forename? 'Wah-keen' would be his usual response. When, as a child, he decided he needed a similar nature-charged moniker to his siblings – River, Summer, Rain and Liberty – he would fend off questions like 'Why Leaf?' by telling a tale of how when he was a four-year-old kid blowing leaves with his father, he decided on his new name. 'My brothers and sisters all had these beautiful names, and I guess I felt a little left out,' he said.

It's his surname, however, for which he became known. From childhood to young adulthood, Joaquin

Phoenix has been, to the world's eye, simply the younger brother of River. It has been the way throughout his life and, tragically, his brother's death at only 23.

River's shadow had loomed large not just over his family members but also over the hearts of teenage girls throughout the eighties and early nineties. It was his teen heart-throb looks, which had earned him the name 'young Elvis' by the all-powerful child-actors' agent Iris Burton after she first clapped eyes on him, and his charismatic delivery in films like *My Own Private Idaho* and *Stand By Me* that captured their hearts.

But it was his death that immortalised River Phoenix. Rightly or wrongly, he would be remembered as one of the movie greats. He would never grow old, or make cuddly, safe films to top up his pension fund. His legacy is rooted in the earth of Hollywood. He had the innocent soul of someone ruined by the business like Marilyn Monroe, and the live-fast die-young rebel spirit of James Dean.

To Joaquin Phoenix, however, he was just a brother – the one that he would share a room with for many, many years, and one half of their apparently dead-on impersonation of Scooby-Doo and Shaggy. There seems to be nothing to suggest any resentment from

Joaquin towards River when they were growing up. In fact he always sought approval and comfort from his older sibling much as a kid would do from his father. But his older brother was exactly that. River's role as an authority figure, and certainly a provider for the family from a young age, marked the sort of role reversal and dysfunctional aura that would mark the Phoenix clan. However, to their credit, they also instilled a set of family values that would bond them together tightly during their many moments of personal drama.

The Phoenix kids would be remembered by many as an all-singing all-dancing clan that entertained their way through the streets handing out religious pamphlets to bemused spectators in Puerto Rico, before the focus moved on to Summer and River attempting to sing for their supper in America, and their attempt to break into Hollywood.

But it was never meant to be that way. The mother and father of this incredibly close-knit family didn't dream of Hollywood success for themselves only to live out that life through their talented brood, like pushy parents throughout the world. The life they were hoping to carve for themselves and their family was a self-contained one, far from the corruption and materialistic world they themselves had grown up in.

Arlyn Dunetz was just a normal Jewish woman, raised by a middle-class family in New York's Bronx and destined for a run-of-the-mill life as a Manhattan secretary in an unloving marriage to a computer programmer. She had other plans, however, and vowed that her life would be different to that of her Hungarian mother Margaret.

Arlyn once said, 'At eighteen I was just a clone, totally unconscious. I didn't know the air was polluted and I didn't care. I just went to work and thought that everything the government told me was right and true. It took some time before I was awakened. I became aware. It was difficult because my parents weren't seeing the same thing, but I knew I had to change my life.'

Her mother predicted that her daughter would end up being a hippy – the then current way to rebel against your family was to join the sixties free-love revolution.

The strict, hard-right hand-wringing section of America was facing, for the first time in its life, a rebellion from its younger citizens.

The deaths of the two Kennedys and Dr Martin Luther King – as well as the Vietnam War, which was in full swing in 1968 – soured the nation. There was a backlash, and it was one that would be accompanied by some of the greatest music ever heard, fuelled by mind-bending drugs and topped off with one of the biggest sexual revolutions America had ever seen.

'It was a time of dissension and conflict in the nation, we were seeking an answer,' Arlyn said.

She formed a simple plan. She would leave her husband, whom she had married shortly after finishing high school, and make a new life for herself – far away from the current lifestyle that was stifling her so much. She wasn't happy, and she believed there was more to life than the nine-to-five jobs and occasional dinner parties she was being subjected to.

The answer would be California. And she would have to hitchhike, which seems out of date now, but in 1968 it was an acceptable and popular mode of transport.

On her many attempts to hitch west to California she met John Bottom – a man who, on surface level at least, was the complete polar opposite to her. He was a high school dropout who seemed content living his life on the road, away from the young daughter that he had left behind. He had suffered a series of personal tragedies whilst growing up. His mother had had a car accident when he was a young boy, the result of which left her brain damaged. His relationship with his father was not a good one. Unable to cope with his wife's medical bills, Ehlia Bottom would turn to drink to get him through it all. But the debts kept mounting up, as the drinking got worse, and it seemed only a matter of time before he would lose his home.

When John was 13 he came home to find that his father was nowhere to be found. He had simply abandoned him. His Aunt Francis would say, 'We went to Church every Sunday – Johnny wanted to go, but he got into trouble. I remember he and another teen tried to set fire to a building. Johnny was sent to a care home, not Juvenile Hall but a place privately owned that cared for errant teens. He was a wild boy. I don't think his parents were that good to the children. They had to root for themselves.'

After his father left him, John Bottom's world was turned upside down – and the subsequent years would see no upturn in his fortunes as he flitted between stays with family members and orphanages. He was to turn to drink and drugs – namely, marijuana. A serious back injury would hinder his attempts to try and earn a living, mostly through carpentry and gardening. The injury was due to a carpentry accident when he was young, or a head-on collision with a car while he was on his bike, depending whether you believe his relatives or John. It would, in fact, be an injury that was to play a big part in River and Joaquin's path to Hollywood.

Fancying himself as a poet and a musical vagabond,

Bottom dropped out of high school to roam around California looking for music work. He would have a daughter named Jodean who was conceived after a brief fling with a woman called Trinity. He had little contact with his daughter, and left for Canada in 1966 over fears he would be drafted for the Vietnam War. Two years later he returned to LA, and soon after he picked up the pretty little hitchhiker that was soon to be his wife.

There was undeniable chemistry between John and Arlyn, and she went back to Bottom's place that night, where they would end up talking for hours about their dreams and how they were fed up with the 'normal life' that everyone wanted for them.

'We were flower children. We were full of faith. We loved everybody,' John would say later, while Arlyn noted, 'We just had similar desires.'

They made it as far as the Pacific Coast, doing things that you would expect free-loving youngsters to do in the sixties. There would be marijuana smoked and acid dropped among the odd jobs they would do along the way. 'We heard that acid was the truth serum. It was the thing that was going to get you above the world, to the level of consciousness where you could feel the power of God,' Arlyn said. They would eventually settle in a farmyard hippie commune later that year, 'marrying' each other during a commitment ceremony performed by the other hippies.

Arlyn and John continued to spring from one commune to another, looking for jobs, but eventually settled on a place called Nance Farm.

Roy Nance told River's biographer Barry C Lawrence, 'I was about twenty-five at the time. She was a pretty little thing. They were about seventeen or eighteen years old when I hired them. They were a rather strange lot. One time I was driving the tractor. The hippies all were supposed to pick up the rocks off the ground and put them into the trailer I was pulling. All of a sudden, it got quiet. I looked back only to find that they all decided to just lay down on their backs and look up at the sun. One of them did that too many times. I still know him, and today he's nearly blind.

'They would take off their clothes and skinny dip at the creek, then lay naked, spread-eagled on the grass, just to shock me. Once I was on the tractor when they did that; I nearly wrecked several rows of potatoes. The women didn't wear any underwear, and they would always bend over whenever I drove by, pretending they were picking something up,' Nance said, going on to describe how he sabotaged their plans to grow marijuana.

'All the hippies planted marijuana seeds here, but I

had put a pre-emergence spray into the soil that they did not know about. So, every time the plants got about an inch high, they would die. They kept wondering why they couldn't grow the stuff, especially since mint grows so well here.

'But, they did work hard.'

Arlyn was pregnant at the time and it seemed a perfect place for them to stay for a while, with Bottom, a skilled gardener, managing to find work harvesting the local mint crop. Despite being pregnant with their first child, Arlyn still helped out by planting potatoes and picking mint. Farmers who remember them during that time would acknowledge how hard they worked, especially the heavily pregnant Arlyn, who rarely complained.

River was born on 23 August, much to the pleasure of not only John and Arlyn – but also to the other couples, who all lived in the same house. Their faces beamed with delight as River was born to the sound of applause by his new house-mates. They all gathered around him at the Oregon home, with a clearly delighted John rushing to the nearest hardware story to look for candles for the naming ceremony.

Nance remembered, 'He was still wet when she walked across the field over to my house to show me the little one, bless his heart. He was still wrapped up in a blanket. He could not have been more than twenty minutes old. I was the first outside person to hold him. He was a cute little bugger.'

An exhausted Arlyn and John would continue to stay at the farm for several more months before deciding they would move once more.

Arriving in Texas, they met a group of young like-minded people, who told the Bottoms about a religious group they had joined. They paid scant attention to the details of this new spiritual movement but enjoyed the group's company and headed to Colorado with them.

With a child in their lives – and with a keenness for more – they were looking for a sense of structure to their daily routine, while still allowing for the liberal and bohemian outlook they both had. Drugs had now become empty and soulless for them and they were seeking more spiritual comfort. Taking their new friends' advice, they found exactly what they were looking for in the shape of the Children of God founder David Berg – or Moses David as he would later call himself. While it would go on to be a controversial movement, at the time it was in its relative infancy, with nearly 150 Children of God groups around the world.

It appeared to be just a simple case of two disillusioned people seeking a community that spoke on their terms, with the Children of God movement answering first. The group preyed on individuals like the Bottoms – promising much about free love and constantly promoting anti-Establishment stance. Later dubbed a sex cult many of its critics, it was clear that sex was a major factor in Berg's vision, and one that would get stronger and stranger as his reign continued.

The prerequisite for any cult leader is charisma, and Berg had it in spades. His rise to that position started from humble beginnings – becoming an evangelist for the Christian and Missionary Alliance in 1964, before roaming around California's Huntington Beach singing folk music and making peanut sandwiches for those who where hungry. In 1968 he founded the controversial movement – which has been under the umbrella of several names, including Teens for Christ, Revolution for Jesus, Family of Love and currently The Family International. But their most famous incarnation is that of Children of God. The cult was a haven for hippies who, like the Bottoms, were striving for meaning and a sense of duty without having to conform or go against their bohemian beliefs; there was a reason it was seen by many as the 'gospel of rebellion'.

Moving back to Texas to the Children of God commune in 1973, the Bottoms quickly set about impressing the leaders of COG.

They began their three-month induction during the Leadership Training sessions at the Texas Soul Clinic

Ranch, during which Berg ensured that everyone knew he was the figurehead of the movement. Their identity of old was being stripped, and a new one given by Berg. Recommending them to rid themselves of their old names, and to take new ones based on biblical figures, Arlyn settled on Jochebed, who was Moses' mother, while John picked the name of the father of Moses, Amram. They worked hard to please their new leaders, eager to seek out the approval of those who mattered.

Berg did not stay with his converts, preferring to live a more suburban life. It was a canny move to bolster his air of mystery and importance and he would only turn up to his convert camps every once in a while. His visits were seen as a huge event: the less people see you, the more impact you have when you turn up. A sense of joy would fill the air whenever word came that Berg was coming.

The Bottoms devoured as much information as they could about the sect, happy too to place their young son in the hands of fellow cult members during daycare sessions. These sessions were like a nightmarish vision of Sunday school. River would be subjected to fiery tales of doom, fire and brimstone warnings of what happened when you sinned; the group foretold a colossal doomsday event following the appearance of the comet Kohoutek, and said that the antichrist would walk this earth destroying the young American children who weren't following Berg's orders. It was all designed to create fear and instill a lasting bond for River to the COG.

By this time, River had a young sister, called Rain, born six days earlier than expected. Her name came from the rainy night that welcomed her into the world. She was delivered by her dad, after Arlyn refused medical help. She would later extend her name to Rainbow when she eleven.

River's time at the camp is shrouded in mystery and controversy. One of the sexual practices Berg preached was that children of a young age should be encouraged to have intercourse. When he was 20, he claimed in an interview that he lost his virginity at around four years old.

'I'm glad I did it when I was young,' he said. 'But, I didn't want those young vaginas and different body parts that were in my face to make me perverse when I was older, so I blocked it out. I was celibate from ten to fourteen. You're just born into that reality, and you accept it.'

Despite later dismissing the comments as nothing but a joke, the damage had been done and soon nameless friends of his who grew up at the same place would claim that he was abused.

River's *Dark Blood* director George Sluizer is quoted as saying, 'He told me quite a lot about his youth. A lot about his childhood – three, four, six years old, eight years old, ten years old. He told me a lot about the sexual abuses.'

Children of God did admit that there was abuse in the higher ranks of the sect, reading out a statement during a court case in the 1990s:

'*[We] acknowledge that any abuse of children is abhorrent, whether it be sexual abuse or other forms of abuse, and we are determined that the Family will be a safe environment for all our children and teens to be brought up in.*

'*We acknowledge that in certain places at certain times the Family has not been as safe an environment for them as it should have been. Over the last nine years, we have taken progressive steps to make it as safe as possible, and have apologised to those who have suffered harm, and we recognise this litigation and these communications as an opportunity to apologise again. We sincerely believe that the Family today is a safe place, and we have established safeguards to make sure it will remain so.*

'*Your Lordship has asked us to acknowledge*

that Father David, through his writings, was personally responsible for children in the Family being sexually abused. Father David wrote a series of Letters concerning sexual behaviour. The judgement refers in particular to "The Law of Love" and "The Devil Hates Sex." And we accept that as the author of ideas upon which some members acted to the harm of minors in the Family, he must bear responsibility for that harm. Maria, and all of us in World Services leadership, also feels the burden of responsibility. Maria in particular has done an enormous amount to put a stop to any sexual maltreatment of children and instituted strict safeguards to make sure it will never happen again.'

The Phoenix clan left their US Children of God base before the height of the sexual controversy that surrounded the cult, and there is no real evidence, bar hearsay and a quote from the actor (who has embellished his past on several occasions), that River was subjected to anything untoward – but the heavy emphasis on sex was the primary reason why the Bottoms eventually left the sect.

Meanwhile, they were to be given a chance to continue preaching the Children of God's teachings elsewhere. They were progressing through the Children of God's ranks, and John was later named the Archbishop of Venezuela. Firstly, though, they headed to Puerto Rico, where they would eventually have their third child. There would be a catch: international members of the Children of God, and especially ones who were flung as far as John and Arlyn, had to fend for themselves. Essentially they were being cut off while still being asked to spread the word – to find those who were as lost as they were and to convert them to the Children of God. On 28 October 1974 Joaquin Rafael Bottom was born.

Speaking in a 1995 interview about the scar on his lip, Joaquin Phoenix noted, 'When my mom was pregnant with me she was in a hammock on the beach and she got these intense pains, and she felt as if some force, God or whatever, had caused this. Then I'm born. A few weeks later she takes me to the doctor, he sees me and says, "Who did this harelip operation? That's the best operation I've ever seen." Mom said, "No one. He wasn't born with a harelip." I was just born with the scar.'

They stayed in Puerto Rico for two more years. Joaquin's earliest memory is being in his dad's arms, floating in the pool his dad tended to, watching iguanas move around.

Money was drying up, however, and with no support from Berg, they decided to head to Venezuela, where they would have a fourth child named Liberty on 5 July 1976.

It would be easy to dismiss the parents of the Phoenix family as hippies and nothing more than a sixties' throwback, but they had a dream of an incredible family unit living day-to-day far away from the perceived corruption of the group. But the cult would use this unit to the full. While adult members were encouraged to undertake a process known as 'provisioning' – a cult member described it as 'asking local businesses for supplies and donations' – the Children of God realised that kids were better sources for attaining money, food and attention for the religious movement. In John and Arlyn's case it helped, of course, that the kids were as adorable as the Bottom brood.

Their older children – River and Rain – would become a source of income for food with their singing in public. Their raw musical shows, with River strumming the handful of chords that he knew, were bolstered by their innate charm, and they drew large crowds at the plaza they played in. He had been taught the guitar by a Spanish singer, and both children seemed natural at charming those that they played for – indeed they would soon be dubbed 'The Blond Children Who Could Sing', the literal translation.

River once said, 'A lot of people would gather and listen to us. It was really a novelty. We had a whole act together. I'd be strumming on the guitar that was taller than I was at about a hundred miles an hour. I knew about five chords. That's where I learned to give a lot of joy and happiness from singing.'

A fellow member of the Children of God, Ado, discussed those days with *US Magazine*: 'It was in Venezuela on Liberty Day in 1976 when they had their second daughter, Liberty Butterfly. They were devoted parents, and we took many camping trips together with our kids. I do remember them telling us that one reason they joined was to stay off drugs.

'Only later did Arlyn and John say that they worried about leading their kids on such a vagabond journey. I reassured them it was a once-in-a-lifetime chance to see the world while doing good work. And when the kids began performing, well, that was something that would always stick with them. It sure paid off.

'Every Friday night, the kids sang in the plaza Candelaria. River and Rain were the stars. River would sing in perfect Spanish. He had great facility on the guitar, which was as big as he was. The boy could attract a crowd,' he recalled.

'We handed out a lot of Jesus pamphlets, mainly for young people, to get them off drugs,' River said. 'My sister and I both sang, I played guitar. I would talk over the microphone…and say, "God loves you" in Spanish…and I really believed it.'

Joaquin would say about his parents, 'I think they were of a generation that was searching, that was discontented. They were very driven for themselves in what they wanted to do. They hoped to have an impact on society and on how we viewed things. Something that I'm always surprised by when I see it, and was shocked by particularly when I was younger, was that with a lot of my friends' parents, the affection, physical contact, and emotional support that I really got from my parents was not present in their lives. The impact that my parents had on me was never anything forced. I never felt that I was being talked down to. An environment of equality was created. I remember my parents talking to all five of us kids about where we'd like to move next. They'd say, "This is a decision that affects the whole family."

'My parents were the ones who were working and who had to find a place for us to live, yet they were very concerned about how we would react to our moves.'

One decision they made would certainly affect the whole family.

Money was getting scarcer to find more than ever, and the Bottoms looked at their squalid shelter in disgust. Essentially cut off from the Children of God, they saw it as a blessing, with Arlyn claiming that the whole notion of 'Flirty Fishing' was the last straw. This referred to the fact that in 1976, Berg essentially advocated that female converts use their sexuality to lure new members to the cult.

Berg's statements and vision for the cult were getting more and more unhinged, with greater onus on sexual intercourse with younger members and even your own relatives; one COG booklet quoted Berg as saying, 'There is nothing in the world at all wrong with sex as long as it is practised in love, whatever it is or whoever it is with, no matter who or what age or what relatives or what manner – and you don't hardly dare even say these words in private.'

Berg's daughter Deborah Davis (born Linda Berg) wrote an exposé of the Children of God, and alleged her father continually attempted to have an incestuous relationship with her. She claimed that her dad told her, 'In the Bible God makes many exceptions to his rules. How do you think Adam and Eve propagated the human race?'

She wrote, 'He railed for hours quoting scripture after scripture to prove his point. Then he turned his attack directly against me. Because I had refused my father's desire for an incestuous relationship. I had in effect refused to accept him as God's Prophet.'

Arlyn would say later, 'The guy running it got crazy. He sought to attract rich disciples through sex. No way.'

Asked about his early days, and recalling his parents time as members of the Children of God, Joaquin would remain defiant, telling *Uncut* magazine in 2001: 'It might have become a cult, but when we were there it was a really religious community. It was a time when people were questioning the nuclear family of the Fifties, people were saying they weren't satisfied with the upbringing their parents had, is there another way? My parents were just searching for an alternative way of raising their children; they didn't want to raise us in the Bronx. My mom was raised in the Bronx, and she was scared every day coming home from school.

'My parents have never been blind followers. In fact, they recognised that it was shifting and the ideas behind it weren't what they wanted, so we left. The awful stuff I've heard about the group in the Eighties, that wasn't our experience. We were trying to figure out how to make alternative societies, and a lot of them fell to the same mistakes that our larger society has made, in which people's egos and greed took over. I think that's what happened to that community. But it wasn't the picture people paint.'

After David Berg died in 1997 'The Family', as they were now called, attempted to address the notoriety surrounding the religious movement. They wrote to former members, saying, 'We hope that former members will try to accept and understand that The Family has changed a great deal over the years. Our general beliefs, message and missionary goal of reaching the world with the Gospel remains the same, of course, but there have been very definite changes of policy which have been made – not for the sake of expediency, but because such change was needed, agreed upon, and implemented.

'Most notably, [Flirty Fishing] has not been in practise since 1987. Sexual contact between adults and minors has been an excommunicable offence since 1986.'

But at that moment, for John and Arlyn, Children of God was no longer an option. As Joaquin noted, it had taken a sudden turn into murky waters and they wanted out. Their choices were limited, but a friend they had met on their travels helped them.

US missionary Father Wood had known the Bottom family for a short time.

'I got to know the Children of God as I was director

of youth ministry for Miranda State, which surrounds Caracas. They were very hot on Jesus. Their leader said to me, "Let's see if we can work together." So we tried, we tried seriously to work together, incorporating them into my work, having presentations. I was going to have a meeting with a group of kids. I said to Children of God, "Why don't you come along, sing a little bit, and see if we would complement each other." A group of about twelve or fifteen of them lived with me in the basement of the cathedral of Los Teques, Venezuela. We tried to work together, but they were on the move so much (that) it was impossible to plan or to do any kind of organised work. It was, for them, very spontaneous. It was what God told them to do that day, or whatever. They had a meeting, and they decided, "It wasn't right for them today," so...and because of certain theological differences and because their interpretation tended to be rather fundamentalist Protestant and very apocalyptic, you know "The end of the world was coming very, very soon", they went their way, I went mine.'

The Bottom clan paid him a visit one day. They were penniless, barely surviving, and now with four mouths to feed they realised they needed help.

Wood is quoted as saying, 'When Arlyn and John showed up one day at my parish door, they told me they decided to leave to follow the Bible, not Moses

23

David. They had no food, no money, no place to stay, no way to get back to America. But they had incredible faith and confidence that God would provide for them.'

Wood took pity on the couple and their adorable brood. He knew of their entertainment skills and so a compromise was agreed upon. They would sing at the Sunday service, and Wood would let them stay with him. This arrangement lasted several months – before they tried fending for themselves, and went to stay, according to River, in a rat-invested beach hut outside the city.

'(It) had no toilets. It was really horrible, but I was never frightened. When you're raised on the road you don't fear these things, you don't question them. We had faith, lots of faith. I don't know the superior Being in the form of a man, woman or jellyfish, but when I think of my parents and their different worlds and how they met and had kids, there has to be be something up there,' River said.

Wood, however, described those surroundings as perfectly adequate, complete with a swimming pool and the idyllic image of the youngsters helping themselves to coconuts and mangos from the trees.

If River did indeed embellish his surroundings every once in a while, it certainly helped his image as the sort of free and sensitive downtrodden spirit that he would be marketed as later in life. As an aside, however, he was actually asked to downplay this side of him at the beginning of his career.

Arlyn could of course have gone to her family, who no doubt would have helped financially, but she wouldn't contemplate that option at that time, certainly not at least until they got back to her homeland. The idea of heading back to the US would be something John and Arlyn discussed several times, eventually realising that it was now the right time to go back to America. However, there was an obvious difficulty in how they could finance their move. They turned again to Father Wood, with John asking for his advice on how to get back to the States.

Wood is quoted as saying, 'While they were definitely poor, it was never quite down to the level of Venezuelan poverty. They were struggling, and they didn't have much money, and she didn't know where they were really going to go.

'I thought to myself, "We are still building the parish, but we do a lot of charity work. We try to help the needy people around town." But I didn't feel I could justify using the parish money for "gringos" to pay their plane fare back to the States.

'Then it suddenly popped into my head, an air plane

is not the only way to get there. You can go by sea. I had in my parish a good number of Basques who were, by nature, seafaring people, and I knew that some were in the shipping business. I went to talk to a maritime captain who was a member of the church and the owner of a small cargo line.'

Wood explained the family's situation, and the captain was sympathetic, especially as he had seen the kids singing at church and, like most people, he thought of them as a cute family unit. There was one room available for the family. Wood was delighted, even pressing his luck to ask whether the cook would make a cake for Joaquin, who was turning four during the trip. The captain happily agreed as he wasn't smuggling illegal immigrants into the country. They were an American family trying to make their way back home.

While River would again embellish the story by claiming that they were stowaways and were discovered halfway through the trip, they were treated well during the voyage. The ship was delivering a shipment of Tonka toys, and, as such, on Joaquin's fourth birthday he was given a huge birthday cake and a Tonka toy as his present. It would be the very first toy he ever had – his face beamed with joy as he held the rarest of things, a present on his birthday.

Joaquin has always been at pains to distance his parents and siblings from the vagabond reputation they have, annoyed that theirs was presented as a dysfunctional family. 'My parents always encouraged us to be expressive. They always supported us, whatever we wanted to do. If you wanted to play the piano, fine, go ahead. If we dressed up in costumes and wrecked my mom's dresses she would just laugh. And my parents were the least judgmental people in the world. I never grew up thinking that person's bad or that person's good. Typically, the people you might look at like criminals were people who gave us a ride. That's what sticks with me the most – all the help we received, all the people who opened their doors and took us in.'

He added, 'I remember birthdays and Christmases where we couldn't afford any presents, so we tried to make them. Lots of times we didn't have much food. But we didn't care, we were kids, you know? My parents always talked to us like adults, they involved us in decisions. When I look back I can't believe how my parents managed, but the cliché is true. We didn't have money, but we were rich in so many other ways.'

Arlyn and John's fourth child, Summer, said much the same: 'We had no money. All we had was each other. It's all you need.'

While the trip brought on exciting and memorable recollections, it also served up an early traumatic memory. An inquisitive Joaquin had crept onto the deck with his family to see the crew at work. It was there that he saw the fishermen haul in their huge catch. He watched open-mouthed as they dropped hundreds of fish onto the deck, and screamed in terror as they writhed about on the ground. Worse was to come for the sensitive four-year-old.

To prevent the fish from slipping off the boat, some were smacked against the wall by the fishermen, to kill them. Minutes before, Joaquin had seen them jumping around in the water, and now they were lying dead next to his feet.

'It was our first concrete experience seeing what happens to "food" before it gets on the table, and we just decided never again to eat anything that had once breathed,' he recalled.

Traumatised, Joaquin begged his parents to never eat anything alive again. Calming her son down, Arlyn insisted that they would indeed become vegetarians – later choosing to cut out dairy products as well, as it was still exploitation of animals.

'The kids were young, and they knew they were giving up pizza, but they wanted to do it for moral reasons. I think if we'd said we were gong to become vegetarians because it's healthier, it would have been difficult. It's definitely a moral thing,' Arlyn said.

It would be a vow to which Joaquin still adheres to this day. Not that he's never slipped up, of course, and even as a kid he would try and steal chocolate bars. He once revealed, 'I don't try to impose my views on anyone else, and I can simply say I feel it's right for me.

'Of course, I've had slips. When I was about twelve I stayed with a friend in San Diego. They got pizza, and I was like, "I'm having some mother-fucking pizza." I ate two slices and vomited for two days.

'I'm strange in that I crave salads and vegetables. I've never really had a sweet tooth, and I don't particularly like foods that are too rich. I'm a parent's dream.'

They eventually arrived in Florida at the end of 1978, with a chance to mark out a new adventure in the States, and stayed with Arlyn's parents, who had moved there from New York. Joseph and Marjorie Dunetz were beside themselves with excitement at seeing their grandchildren.

It was an emotional reunion for those who had met before, and hugs aplenty for those clasped for the first time. At four years old, Joaquin finally set foot on American soil and he was already surrounded with joy and love.

It was to be a learning process for the family. A

shocked Marjorie demanded that River be enrolled in school straight away – a completely alien concept to River, then aged seven, and who at this point had only been home-schooled.

Someone who would have a big impact on the children's lives, Gus Van Sant, said, 'He [River] had lived such a strange life. He once told me that he didn't know what a joke was until he was nine, and he was in a public school all of a sudden and someone told a joke, and he didn't know the form. He knew about laughter, and funny things, but had never heard of a joke.'

They would once again be fishes out of water. But John Bottom was hopeful – he was back home, family in tow.

For Joaquin, his American adventure had begun.

CHAPTER TWO

TURN OVER
A NEW LEAF

Joaquin – or Leaf, as he would now be known, because 'My brothers and sisters all had these beautiful names, and I guess I felt a little left out' – was, as he had admitted, 'a little terror'. He was a constant bundle of energy and mischief – claiming that all he wanted to do was 'break windows and stuff'. He would say that he was the one who would make the babysitters cry, and the one who would wind down the windows in the car when everyone else was cold. But Joaquin was also the sort of boy that rather than just passing a homeless person would sit down and chat to him for ages. Martha Plimpton, who dated River for a long period and starred with Joaquin in *Parenthood* (1989), said, 'He was always physical and really emotional.'

River summarised his siblings during promotion of *The Mosquito Coast*: 'We all look completely different from each other and we all have our distinct things. Leaf was the family clown, the comedian – very witty and smart. Rainbow was the older sister and trendsetter. Mom had to work a lot, so she took her place. I played the guitar… I went off to my room a lot and had a real goofy side to me, really corny – laughing about stupid things, making fart noises with my mouth. A lot of inside jokes. Liberty was always the most physical, like an acrobat – nimble, strong, slender, a really beautiful girl. And Summer was the youngest, the baby of the family, with big brown eyes and blonde hair. She looks WASPy. Liberty and Rainbow have more of an ethnic look – Israeli or Italian.'

Settling in the States, John found work as a gardener, with his 12- to 16-hour days ensuring that his family's mouths were fed. And there was yet another addition to the family: Summer Joy was born on 10 December 1978 – the Joy representing how they were feeling as a family unit back in America. They stayed with Arlyn's parents at first but soon realised their house was too small for them all.

The musician who had given River his first guitar,

Alfonso Sainz, told John and Arlyn that if they ever moved to Florida they should meet up with him. They promptly did, half hoping perhaps that Alfonso could help River with a music career.

While that was never to materialise, he suggested that John and his family stay in his caretaker's house, providing that John took care of the place as a handyman – something that delighted his kids, who would regularly help their father out, either by carrying dirt or helping to put in plants. The place may not have been the same in scope and size as the mansion Sainz himself lived in, but to the Bottom clan it was like a castle.

One of the neighbourhood children said, 'I spent the night at their house a few times. Their parents would tell us goodnight stories, but they were really trippy – about the stars and all. Then, they [John and Arlyn] would sneak out of the house and go and visit their hippie neighbours. So they were not afraid to leave their kids alone. The kids were free to do what they wanted. My parents would not have let me stay there if they'd known we were left alone.'

The children were happy, despite River finding it a bit difficult to fit in at school.

However, disaster struck the family three months later when John aggravated his old back injury to such an extent that it made it impossible for him to continue gardening.

Seizing upon the experiences they learned from being in the Children of God – namely that children were far more likely to appeal to charitable passer-bys than adults – they realised that in nine-year-old River and two years younger Rain they had two children who were well versed in showmanship despite their tender ages. And they were in America – the land of talent contests.

Father Wood remembered, 'I got the feeling that parents in the Children of God were exploiting their kids' talents, aware that the kids were more effective beggars than them. Over the years, as we stayed in touch, Arlyn and John would explain, "We manage our kids' careers," but I always felt ambivalent with that dynamic. Once they left the cult, they never had any profession except for being the parents of these talented progeny.'

Sure enough, River and Rain would be a constant fixture on the talent-show circuit, and it wouldn't be long before they were being placed in first position. As big fish in a small pond, they were featured in the local papers. When asked if they wanted to be famous, Rain replied, 'I don't want to get rich. I want to give money to poor people and some for us. I like to give to people who need help.'

River meanwhile, replied, 'I hope to be famous someday, not to be proud of myself, but because I thank God for giving me my powers.'

Florida wasn't the right place for them if they wanted their talents nurtured. Hollywood was where they needed to be and, in Arlyn, they had a contact. A girl she knew at high school was having huge success as an actress in the television show *Laverne & Shirley*. The actress in question, Penny Marshall, was shown some newspaper reports about the talented family, and promptly gave them to a Paramount employee who, in turn, suitably impressed, said that if the family should ever be in LA they should come by – but made it clear that they were not to come especially to see them.

The Bottoms, however, saw it as a sign that Hollywood was their calling. Arlyn would later claim that 'We had the vision that our kids could captivate the world'.

Handing out pamphlets in Venezuela in a bid to convert people was one thing, but could the Bottom children make it in the entertainment industry? They certainly believed so, months before they had changed their surname to Phoenix in reference to new hope – and this was to prove the vindication of it.

In John's words: 'We sold everything, and moved to LA.'

They set off on their 3,000-mile trip, like the flower-power version of *The Beverly Hillbillies*. The children were all crammed into the back of a beat-up old Volkswagen van, with taped together nappies replacing the back window, and River telling all that he met on their way at petrol stations that he was going to become a Hollywood star.

They drove to the only other family members that mattered to John – his Aunt Francis and Uncle Beck. They had looked after him for a time following his dad's abandonment. After getting over the shock of seeing her nephew after all these years, Francis doted on the young ones. She said, 'They were strict vegetarians, they had gotten into this way of eating. They won't eat meat, they won't wear anything made out of cowhide – everything had to be cloth or plastic.

'I had to fix them either a fruit or vegetable platter; they would not eat the two together. It was either one or the other. River came in the kitchen. He said, "Aunt Francis, we can't eat but one." Okay, well, eat this one, and then you can take the other home,' she replied. 'They spent the night in their old beat 'em up camper before they left for Hollywood the next day. They didn't have hardly anything. We just tried to help them out.'

While the kids expected to strap on a guitar and sing

their way into a Hollywood career, Arlyn knew they would have to work hard and hope for some luck. They would be on the move constantly, with little time spent forging new friendships. But a large family and the close confines they lived in would ensure they never got lonely. They were poor, that much was in no doubt, but their parents would turn it into a big adventure. Joaquin remembers having to sneak into their small apartment, carefully treading past signs that stated, 'No kids, no dogs'.

On one occasion he was caught by the landlady that lived above them. However, instead of throwing him out, she handed him an *Incredible Hulk* doll. 'We always had angels in our lives – people who become friends and are friends to this day,' he said.

Speaking about their closeness, Joaquin recalled during an interview in 2000, 'I was just at my friend Casey (Affleck's) place and Jake Paltrow was over, and I was hugging and saying goodbye to my sister, Summer; she was going to Los Angeles for a couple days. And Jake said, "Oh, it's so nice to see siblings that have that kind of interaction and that closeness; that's what I have with Gwyneth." But to me it's just how things have always been, so it doesn't seem like a big deal. We're all like a year-and-a-half apart, so there's just a connection from the top to the bottom. We always had each other.'

When they had to leave their temporary home, sometimes they would sleep in their van, or would head back to Aunt Francis one more time.

She is quoted as saying, 'I know they didn't have anything, didn't have beds – they slept on the floor. I got a mattress for them. I finally found the frame, and I called him up, and said, "Johnny, if you want a frame for your bed, come out here, I have one for you."

'Anything I had – kitchen utensils, or anything, they wanted it. They didn't even have clothes. When we would visit them, we'd go in on a Sunday. We'd gather up vegetables and things and take them to them, so they'd have food to eat. Christmas, we took them gifts and everything, but they didn't accept gifts. I took them all the things for decorating their Christmas tree and everything. They said they weren't going to have a tree. In fact, some neighbour brought 'em over a Christmas tree, but they didn't deserve it. They didn't believe in it.'

The Penny Marshall connection ultimately didn't work out – although the family did get to meet *Happy Days*' The Fonz – played by Henry Winkler – for their troubles.

Their options were running out, and fast. They figured on one last throw of the dice to grab their new life and, ironically, it would see Arlyn use her skills from her previous life. Before she met John Bottom she was a more than competent secretary, and she figured that by getting a job at a major studio in a secretarial position she had a greater chance of finding suitable contacts for her children.

She didn't make a nuisance of herself, however. Producer David Gerber, who would go on to give River, and ultimately Joaquin, his big break by casting River in *Seven Brides for Seven Brothers*, said of her time with him, 'She was wonderful. She worked at the studio and we were close. She made sure my calls went in and handled all my meeting appointments. She looked after me real good. However, she never tried to influence anything. In fact, I was surprised to find out that he was her son. I really respected her. She was never overbearing or pushy.'

Still, it was a plan that was ultimately a masterstroke. She managed to get a job at NBC as the secretary for casting director Joel Thurm, who in turn introduced Arlyn to the one and only children's agent Iris Burton

Not too shy to brag about her standing in Hollywood – the title 'Legendary Iris Burton' was self-proclaimed – Burton's confidence was justified. She would regularly feature in the Hollywood power lists, and with good reason. If you saw a kid or a young teenager in an advert there was a good chance they worked for Burton. As for high-profile clients – she would oversee the careers of the Olsen twins, the Duff sisters, Fred Savage, Josh Hartnett and Kirsten Dunst.

As such, she was revered by studio bosses and producers – her office was packed with invites to lavish premieres and networking parties, while her desks were covered in flowers, fruits and candy. Studios were scared to put child actors on the rosters – mainly due to their reluctance to deal with their mothers – but she knew exactly what she was doing: making sure that her kid actors earned adult wages. She was successful because clients preferred Burton's kids – they didn't have the 'staginess' of others.

She once said, 'By the time a kid walks through that door I know if he or she's a winner or a loser. If they jump in or slouch in, if they're biting their nails or rocking back and forth, I don't want them. If I don't see the hidden strength, feel the energy, then the magic isn't there. I can smell it like a rat. I hate saying it, but kids are pieces of meat. I've never had anything but filet mignon. I've never had hamburger – my kids are the choice meat.'

Dismissing suggestions she was an agent, she once said, 'I'm a child groomer, a talent scout. I don't like the kids to be too well trained. I watch their weight, their hair. And most of all, I watch their parents.'

Talking about Iris, Joaquin said in an interview in 1998, 'Oh, I've been with her my whole career. I got with her when I was about six years old. My whole family has been with her. She was the only agent that took all of us. We went to a number of agents that said, "OK, we'll take Rain and Summer but we won't take Liberty, River or Joaquin." We didn't want to be split up. My parents wanted us all together, and we went in and met her and she loved all of us and took us all. She's just a really sweet, great woman who works on her own.

'Her office is a room behind her house. She believes in me and believes that I can do anything, so I don't have to deal with package deals and agents going, "Well, Joaquin's not really that type. We see him more as this, but we could get so-and-so."'

He went on, 'You know, at the big agencies I think they have these kind of power meetings. I don't know because I've never been there, but this is my assumption. They have these meetings where they say, "We have this script from this writer and I think that so-and-so is the type of part." I mean, I grew up with her. She's part of the family, so it's actually a great relationship and I've never been pressured into doing anything. She can be very strong-minded about certain projects: "I really think you should do this." But we always manage to agree on all of my choices, and I'm really happy with my career.'

With Arlyn desperate to have all the kids with the same agency, it might seem that you had to take the whole package to get River, but all the Phoenixes had their own unique abilities, particularly Joaquin. Even then he had these deep-set eyes, filled with wide-eyed wonder that seemed perfect for the screen. They would grab the attention of anyone who saw him, be it teachers, friends or his parent's pals, long before he would become a screen idol.

In his book *Hunting With Barracudas*, Burton's assistant Chris Snyder wrote, 'Iris had taken on the whole family and worked around them being vegans and not wearing leather. That left them out of a majority of the commercial work available to kids, but Iris didn't care. She saw something in those kids. Iris fought for her clients and she became very involved with them. She went on vacations with them, shared holidays with them and in some instances stayed as a guest in their holiday homes.'

Joaquin added, 'Iris immediately found something interesting in each individual. She's a wonderful woman, very maternal. And our options for work were limited because we wouldn't do any commercials for Coca-Cola or McDonald's or meat or milk or anything like that. The first thing my agent said to our parents was, "These kids are just starting out, and you're already telling me that eighty per cent of all the commercials out there, they're not gonna do? You're leaving yourself nothing here," but she still took us.'

Despite having an agent, and being in a number of ads, River's acting career hadn't quite taken off the way everyone expected. A year went by and still they were looking for that elusive part. There would be the occasional job but not enough to sustain the large family. And so the children were still doing their performances in shopping centres in a bid to earn some money.

However, Arlyn was still convinced they would get the big chance they were desperate for. She believed that everything they had gone through as a family – hunger, constant travelling, sailing on a ship and many many nights of wondering where the next source of income would be coming from – had all been about getting to this place.

She talked about this in 1988: 'Whatever the connection was that kept us through that time is still keeping us through this time. Because the success and the money and the fame and all of that aren't really important to us. Aren't as important as accomplishing the mission of doing it, because we felt this is what

God was leading us to do. And, the children have the talent and everything to go with it. I mean, River has his own drive to do what has to be done, and God willing, he will come out unspoiled. And, maybe by some other miracle, we can use whatever we've gained to enlighten and help the whole world, not just our family.'

Her faith would finally be rewarded, with the news in 1982 that River had landed the role of the youngest male son in the family TV series *Seven Brides for Seven Brothers*. Based on the 1954 Hollywood film, the part-drama, part-musical show focused on a parent-less family of rowdy brothers. Among its stars was Richard Dean Anderson – who would go on to have big success on the TV show *MacGyver*.

News that River had landed the part understandably caused a huge level of excitement in the Phoenix household – with River exclaiming, 'I just leaped five foot into the air. I got all red faced and freaked out. It was my first television show, real exciting. A glorious moment. It's something I just waited for, and it's such a rare thing, being at the right place at the right time and just fitting the part. I liked it a lot better than commercials, which I didn't like at all.'

To celebrate, the Phoenix family would move once more, this time to a three-bedroom house and five acres of land in a Californian town called Murphys. It was something of a shock to the system for the Phoenix children, who would visit their now famous brother on set. While they were in awe of the sets and lavish musical numbers, the shock to River's system was a different one. Apart from some time at a state school, this was the first real time he found himself surrounded by people that didn't share the same beliefs as his family and their like-minded friends.

Producer Gerber remembers getting a call from those involved in the series, telling him that they had a big problem. 'His parents didn't want River to wear leather. And, when you're doing a western you have to wear cowboy boots made out of leather. That was not ideologically acceptable to them. It put River in a very uncomfortable position as a kid, but what could he do except obey his parents.'

A frustrated Gerber told his production team that River didn't have to wear a leather belt, telling them to give him some rope instead. It quickly became clear to the show's cast and crew that the young child beside them wasn't quite like them, and he soon became the object of ridicule. Some claim that the teasing River was subjected to was merciless and done with some malice. Others, however, believe it was just a case of normal banter, but one that wasn't dealt with well by

River because he had no idea how to cope with such an alien concept.

Gerber told Barry C Lawrence, 'He was a juvenile, young kid, and they had fun with him. They would tousle his hair, they would kid around because he's a young kid. However, I never had any director or my producer call me up and say that there were problems. None I know with River. He was such a good kid.

'I think they were probably just kidding him about his veganisim and his no-animal stuff. However, I do not think it was malicious. We had Jimmy Brown, who is a very tough producer, a fine producer. He would not let anybody do anything like that. He just would not let that happen. We never heard of anything. I think it was [just a case of] playing around with the kid, you know, having fun. They were nice kids. They all acted like one unit, like one family.'

Actress Martha Plimpton, however, would say, 'I love River's family. They brought him up to believe he was a pure soul who had a message to deliver about the world. But in moving around all the time, changing schools, keeping to themselves and distrusting America, they created this utopian bubble so that River was never socialised. He was never prepared for dealing with crowds and with Hollywood.'

While the show would only run from September

1982 to March 1983, it was clear that River was something of a star, attracting a huge legion of female fans. 'We got heavy fan mail for River,' Gerber said. 'The young girls really liked him, and we started giving him a bigger role in the show because he was so popular.' His parents told him to reply to each letter personally, something he was only too happy to do.

Despite the show not being picked up for a second season, River would establish himself as someone to watch. And over the next two years he found steady work.

River was the star of the family, and also the breadwinner. He would tell his *Explorers*' co-star Ethan Hawke not long after, 'I'm going to be famous. Definitely. Rich and famous.' When asked why, River replied, 'I'm doing it for my family.'

Hawke would add, 'After that night, I really saw the heavy trip his family laid on him. To them, he was the Second Coming, the man of the house at age fourteen. Maybe that's why River always took himself so seriously.'

River was serious business, however, and yet still Joaquin was not in awe of his sibling. He had no huge desire to be an actor himself, and was happy to let his brother take centre stage. In fact, Joaquin claims that he never realised just how famous his brother was –

what with living in a small town and not having a TV or reading celeb magazines.

'I don't think I had really been aware of the fame that my brother had acquired, because he never carried himself as such. Our television at home had only one channel, and it was PBS. I never saw premieres, never watched *Entertainment Tonight*, any of that. So his celebrity was another world, and when that world was suddenly brought to our doorstep, I think it just rocked me. You just want to go through your own process of acceptance, or understanding – if there is any – without any other influences. Through all that I hadn't seen much that was positive. I mean there certainly was an outpouring of love from a lot of people, but more than anything, there was a lot of ugliness.'

Nonetheless, he would find himself thrust into that world soon enough, and would soon be carving a career, however minor at that point, of his own.

'Initially, it wasn't a conscious effort to start acting. My brother had been working on a TV series in northern California, and there were guest spots and my sisters and me got the roles, so I kind of fell into it,' he said.

Indeed, while River had acting, Leaf – or Joaquin – wasn't quite sure where his skills lay. He would try painting and poetry, before conceding, 'You know how you write something when you're young and you like it and you read it like five days later and you're like, "What the hell was that?" That's me.'

School wasn't a particularly happy time, and Joaquin eventually dropped out in the ninth grade. One moment still rankles with him. 'A lot of it made me angry, and the final straw, man, I'm doing this home-school thing and the motherfuckers send a dead bloated frog to my house to dissect.'

He would eventually fall into acting when the producers of *Seven Brides for Seven Brothers* needed a young boy and a girl in an episode. Talent notwithstanding, the idea of casting Joaquin and Liberty, who were on location anyway, was an easy one; they had met them before and it would mean they wouldn't have to undertake a potentially lengthy casting process.

They starred in the thirteenth episode of the show – entitled 'Christmas Song', which aired on 22 December 1982. He would play Travis in the episode, and straight away knew that acting was for him. 'I've always felt when I was younger that there was something missing. I guess you go through that growing up – you want something. As soon as I started working as an actor, I just felt this void had filled,' he said.

Bit parts in the TV drama *Six Pack* and sitcom *Mr*

Smith would follow, before he ended up grabbing a celebrated TV special, as River's younger brother in an ABC Afternoon Special, *Backwards: The Riddle of Dyslexia*. It would be a lead role for River, and a supporting one for Leaf. This was something he would get used to for a while, but it's the sort of role that the Phoenix family wanted the kids to do. While incredibly dated, the very fact that it was a programme dealing with the subject of dyslexia would have fitted in with Arlyn and John's idea for the work they should be doing. John would later voice his frustrations at films that his young brood attached themselves to if he thought that they were servicing Hollywood corruption, but they were happy with River's main character, who dealt with the problems of dyslexia. Aired only once, it became popular in schools, with several US libraries stocking the film for education purposes.

It would be easy to praise, however naïve it may be, John and Arlyn's vision – but it also served them well. The pair stood out from the crowd, and they were free of any stage-parent accusations. Arlyn once said, 'My husband John and I have been blessed with five extraordinary children. I look at them sometimes and wonder why they're mine. Maybe someday we can make a difference in the world.'

Joaquin and River not only got to share some screen time, they were both nominated for young actors' awards. While River showed an easy-going charm, Joaquin's (or Leaf as he was credited for most of his screen performances then) acting was more mannered. He was of course younger than River, and hadn't quite the same level of experience. But he was learning, and there was definite potential. His natural energy on screen was clearly evident.

Like River, he would be used in adverts – recalling a He-Man' advert, Joaquin said, 'I was Skeletor. Somewhere I knew how fake it was. So I'm sitting there actually analysing the little script – you know, in the truest way, Why does Skeletor have pain? I wanted him to be happy. But I realised I couldn't go in there and ask about Skeletor's pain, so I just hammed the fuck out of it, got the part, and never did another commercial again.'

His performances would improve as the roles piled on over the years, such as starring in shows like *The Fall Guy*, *Hill Street Blues* and TV movie *Anything for Love*.

He also had a notable role in *Murder, She Wrote*, which saw Angela Lansbury's Jessica Fletcher travel to Chicago to see her niece and her two children (played by Leaf and his real life sister Summer). Taking the kids on a seemingly uneventful trip to an amusement park, Fletcher inevitably ends up having to solve a complicated murder. (One of the more amusing scenes in the episode sees Leaf's character demand a second serving of hamburgers, his favourite apparently. Of course, you never see him eating one!)

A recurring role in the hour-long drama series *Morningstar/Eveningstar* in 1986, which also starred Burton's client Fred Savage, followed and it seemed it wouldn't be long before Joaquin would be making his appearance on the big screen.

Director Harry Winer was casting for a young boy for his teen fantasy *SpaceCamp* (1986) and was immediately blown away by this 'innocent and enthusiastic' boy who came before him. Winer remembers firstly 'marvelling over his name, further marvelling after hearing the names of his siblings, who were clearly coming from the same tree, as you will'.

Winer added, 'He just had this outgoing personality interestingly enough, was very warm and had this enthusiasm that we were looking for. I think Iris brought in Leaf because he had been so exposed to it because his siblings had been doing it, and he would take to it quite easily. We were looking for an innocence, wide enthusiasm and a vivid imagination – someone you would believe to be into *Star Wars* lock, stock and barrel. Iris certainly delivered the goods.'

The role was of a 12-year-old boy named Max, who

is the youngest recruit to a summer space camp – which teaches teenagers the basics about being astronauts. It was based on the space camp in Alabama. Of course, this being an eighties romp, Max ends up befriending a robot who, in turn, decides to help with young Max's wish to be up in space. Through a series of convoluted events, he ends up sending Max and a group of other teenagers into space.

It's a charming and diverting film – buoyed by Phoenix's big screen debut.

Avoiding the staged expressions and tics that would hinder other young performers, he was certainly growing in each performance, with his acting style becoming less mannered, and showing flashes of the nervous, insular intensity which would become his trademark.

'I guess it was this space that our parents created for us to be creative in,' Joaquin said in an interview. 'We were always encouraged to express ourselves. We spent our days talking and singing and we were always in front of an audience. It wasn't what they call "normal" growing up. We started off singing at children's hospitals and in jails and things like that in Central America. Then we moved to the States – at some point we started singing on the streets in Westwood. We'd be these five kids singing all these songs in front of crowds.'

He added in an interview in 2000, 'I think that you find in a very tight family, where the siblings are close emotionally and in age, that you just tend to follow in the footsteps of your older siblings. You just adopt what the others are doing even if it's listening to music or skateboarding or whatever. We all used to sing and play music, and we were all very outgoing. My parents always encouraged us to express ourselves. And so it seemed like second nature to start acting.'

'He was so open,' said Winer. 'You give him a direction and he will run with it no hesitation. On the one hand when you're that age that just comes with the territory because you haven't learned any bad habits and you haven't learned to have a filter up, so you'll play the game and commit to it completely. But he's an obvious talent.'

Being the young one on set (he was still only 12) might have been a problem but actors like Tate Donovan, Lea Thompson and Kelly Preston treated Leaf like a younger brother. Unlike the problems River faced on *Seven Brides and Seven Brothers*, Leaf was never teased for his upbringing, although it would be fair to say, he was brought up in far less intense circumstances. He joined in with the banter and was part of the cast and crew. In return he helped sell the film's story, with his genuine enthusiasm, ensuring that the older actors stayed rooted in the film's fantasy setting.

'They were all great to him. They loved this kid. Having someone who played with this fantasy – it was easy for them. They took him under their wings like a younger brother and son,' Winer remembered.

It was a fun environment, and Winer remembers having no problems with Leaf at any point during filming – bar one incident. 'This sort of gives you an insight into Joaquin. As I said, he was an open book and you could write into it whatever you wished and he would deliver in the most charming and honest way. There was this scene about weightlessness, and he was supposed to come out of the compression area, which leads into the cargo bay. We had to put him on wires and turn the set on a 90-degree angle and lower him into the cargo bay.

'So he was hung on wires forty feet above the stage. As you can imagine, it was a big production, a lot of people counting on getting the shot done as quickly as possible so they could move on to the next one.'

However, the young Joaquin broke down and refused to do the shot. 'He was terrified and so the money counters are counting money, the production manager is counting time and I'm just trying to talk to this sweet boy to try and convince him, and give him the courage to fly forty feet in the air and have some fun with it – to see the wonders of space for the first time, you know. But every time I spoke to him, he would just break down in abject tears.

'It just so happened that River turned up on set that day, and so it was at this very moment that River came over. I have this image in my mind not of the River of great fame and great potential as an artist, but of an older brother taking a younger brother in his arms. He stooped down on his knees and the two of them would whisper for a few moments together. And this sort of confidence that Leaf gained from his older brother, but also because River had been through the hoops, somehow gave Joaquin something to latch onto, something that would get him over his fear.'

Winer continued: 'River stands up, he's done having a little chat with his brother – Leaf looks over at me with some sense of determination, I say, "Are you ready?" He nods, and boom, he's lifted forty feet off the stage floor and gives us the shot we need and want, and delivers it beautifully without another tear shed. So whatever was said between those two boys, it provided the confidence and strength needed to get that shot done.'

Joaquin would call himself a 'chubby fucker' in the film, joking that he was more interested in the craft service than the actual film. He alleged that he gained a lot of the weight and that 'the producers were getting nervous'.

While filming *SpaceCamp* Joaquin discovered that the set next door was being used by Michael Jackson. The youngster was delighted to be able to meet up with him, not just because he was arguably the most famous music star on the planet, but because he was also a vegetarian.

'There's someone like me! I was like, "Hey dude, here's a cookbook. Merry Christmas."'

It would presumably be *The Cook Book for People Who Love Animals* – the source of many of the Phoenix children's favourite food. One journalist reported on seeing the youngsters squeal with delight as their mother turned to page 42 to make their favourite – Tofu Cheesecake.

The film would eventually gross $9.6 million – a box office failure, considering its estimated $20 million budget. Whether or not they could have used the young Joaquin more in the promotion of the film is debatable. However, a real life tragedy made the marketing people nervous about how to actually sell the film.

'Oh Lord,' said Winer. 'I must say we had other issues, which included the *Challenger* blowing up on the January or February before it opened in the spring or summer. We had some major PR issues everybody was focusing on, like not sending Joaquin into the media. I don't think we used him as effectively as we could have. It was hard to sell a fantasy after there had been such a tragedy.'

The Space Shuttle *Challenger* disaster on 26 January saw the craft break apart after a minute into its flight, killing all of the seven crew members. The incident shocked the nation, and so a feelgood spacecraft romp was hardly something they would be desperate to see, but it hardly wowed the critics either.

Esteemed critic Roger Ebert conceded, 'The great looming presence all through this movie is the memory of the *Challenger* destroying itself in a clear, blue sky. Our thoughts about the space shuttle will never be the same again, and our memories are so painful that *SpaceCamp* is doomed even before it begins. The time is not right for a comedy thriller about a bunch of kids who are accidentally shot into orbit with their female teacher. It may never be right again.'

But he would also note that while the actual premise is promising it's also pretty dumb. And it was an opinion shared with most critics.

Soon after, Leaf starred in *Russkies* (1987) – a cute and disarming story of three American children who come across a Russian sailor.

It was a change of pace from other films of that era – while films like *Red Dawn* focused on a plot about American kids having to cope with a Russian invasion, *Russkies* painted a cautionary tale of paranoia and fear around people being different.

It was a liberal-minded film, and it was a hugely charming if very 1980s piece – think *The Goonies* meets *The Iron Giant*. It was also Joaquin's best performance yet. He was clearly progressing as an actor, seeming to inhabit the roles in both *SpaceCamp* and *Russkies* with a sense of wonder – completely selling both movies' fantasy premise.

More importantly, he was becoming an actor in his own right – dismissing any future suggestions that he was being cast because of his famous brother. It would also see him play the group's leader – a role that he seemed naturally at ease with, but one you would hardly see him play on screen; he normally played an outsider.

Russkies was generally well received by critics. While they would acknowledge its flaws, they were also quick to acknowledge that it was a kind-hearted movie, with Ebert noting, 'The scenes between the Russian and the kids are the best part of the movie, partly because the kids are so well cast. Their natural leader is played by Leaf Phoenix whose brother River accepted a similar assignment in *Stand By Me*, a film that *Russkies* resembles in more ways than one.'

In the nineties he muttered to a journalist who had seen both *SpaceCamp* and *Russkies* that he felt sorry for him. It could have been nothing more than a disarming attempt at self-deprecation, but an MTV interview with Joaquin during promotion of *Reservation Road* (2007) showed him frustrated about being reminded of *SpaceCamp*.

'I actually value every second of everything I have done because it has led me to where I am today. I don't think about it, I haven't thought about it until you brought it up, thanks very much. I have no regrets about my career.' When the interviewer pressed on, with the question, 'What is it about that Robot?' Joaquin snapped, 'Enough of this, I know you want to have a good time, but enough is enough.'

CHAPTER THREE

FLIGHT OF
THE PHOENIX

The Phoenix family were flying high in Hollywood. River's career was going smoothly, and *A Night in the Life of Jimmy Reardon* was set to be released; Rain was making her debut in *Maid to Order*, while Summer and Leaf had *Russkies*.

Talking about the Phoenix brood, River's *Little Nikita* director Richard Benjamin said in 1987, 'They are talented kids. And their parents have instilled in them a sense of morality.'

That sense of morality was the reason why they would have to move again.

Despite their success (River in particular was becoming a Hollywood star ever since he hugely impressed in the classic *Stand By Me*), John was becoming disillusioned with what Hollywood was doing to his children – particularly River.

River said, 'My father is worried that we could be ruined by this business. It's got a lot of pitfalls and temptations, and he doesn't want us to become materialistic and lose the values we were brought up believing in. Yes, he's pleased we're doing well, but in a way he's almost reached a point where he could just drop out again, like he did in the sixties, and move to a farm and get close to the earth.'

Arlyn said, however, 'Show business won't spoil the family. I really think there is a purpose why all this is happening to us. We just have to be patient and let that purpose find us.'

River was diplomatic about the situation, saying, 'That's what I've been explaining to my father. There's a part of me that wants to walk away from all of this, and stop thinking about myself and my career and what film I should do next. But, I also have to fulfil myself and push myself, and find out just now what I'm capable of. Basically, I'm very open about my career right now. I'm not afraid of rejection. But part of me would be happy to quit while I'm ahead, perhaps even go off into the jungle like Allie Fox [a *The Mosquito Coast* character] for a while, and just live off the earth.'

While Arlyn had worked tirelessly in a Hollywood studio trying to kick-start her children's entertainment careers, there was a suspicion John wasn't quite so media savvy. River tried to laugh it off, saying, 'My dad, well, he gets funny sometimes.' But you could see the kid was hurt and embarrassed.

It was John's time to get hurt and embarrassed, by the similarities between himself and River's screen father character in *The Mosquito Coast* – played memorably by Harrison Ford.

River would play the son of a brilliant inventor, a man who is aghast at the superficial lifestyle he has become accustomed to in America. The man rages, 'We eat when we're not hungry, drink when we're not thirsty. We buy what we don't need and throw away everything that's useful. Why sell a man what he wants? Sell him what he doesn't need. Pretend he's got eight legs and two stomachs and money to burn. It's wrong. Wrong, wrong, wrong.'

His plan is to live in utopia, based on his singular dream that an untainted world will give them the richness of life they can't get in a highly populated and hugely corrupted environment.

No wonder that director Peter Weir was considering River, despite the fact that he was too old for his original idea for the character. They were looking for a 12–13-

year-old boy to play the role, with River's *Stand By Me* co-star Will Wheaton being seriously considered.

Nonetheless, his casting director told him, 'There's a boy on this tape. His name is River Phoenix. He's terrific – only he's fifteen.'

River's childhood nagged at Weir, knowing full well that the dramatic potential of one of the actors drawing on such parallel experiences as his character could only be a good thing. There was also the simple fact that he kept going back to River's audition in his head.

It was clear enough to Weir. River Phoenix would play Harrison Ford's son in the movie.

'I finally said to myself, What the hell does it matter how old he is. He looks like Harrison's son and I cast him,' he said on the film's production notes. 'He has the look of someone who has secrets. There's something in him and it goes onto film. The last time I remember seeing it in someone unknown was with Mel Gibson.'

River loved working with the movie star, saying, 'Harrison was down to earth. I had read that he was cold, but he was actually very warm. It's just that in his position you have so many phony people trying to dig at you that you've got to have a shield up. He's a very nice man, wise and practical. His ideals are very practical, logical. I learned a lot from him.

'The biggest thing about Harrison is that he makes acting look so easy, he's so casual and so sturdy. I had a great time working with him. We dealt with each other on an honest level. I understood where he was coming from and I think he understood where I was coming from.'

Ford would reply in kind, saying, 'What he has is some manner of natural talent. There are a lot of people who have that, but River is also very serious about his work. [He's] very workmanlike and professional, far beyond what you'd expect from a fifteen-year-old boy. River asks a lot of questions that require answers, none of which I can really supply but they're interesting questions.' He went on, 'Some of his views were unconventional by today's standards. They made him seem as if he was on a different planet. But even so, you felt he had his feet firmly on the ground.'

The pair seemed to bond on the film, and River would reunite with him on *Indiana Jones and The Last Crusade*. (Well, it wasn't really a reunion on screen as he played the younger version of the famed screen adventurer, but they would spend time together making sure River perfected the mannerisms).

'I would just look at Harrison, he would do stuff and I would not mimic it, but interpret it younger. Mimicking is a terrible mistake that many people do when they play someone younger or with an age difference. Mimicking does not interpret true, because you just can't edit around it.'

Ford in return would spend hours with Phoenix making sure that he got the physicality of the part just right, as well as showing him some of the bullwhip moves.

'I don't think I nagged him. I didn't ask him all the time how Indiana Jones was. I learned a lot from him. Harrison came out and he helped me a lot with motivation. You know, where does all this come from and what propels, and what makes him really cool when he has to jump off a horse onto a train.'

While Leaf was wrestling with the dilemma of what to do about his stuttering acting career (more of that later), the Hollywood blockbuster fan was delighted to see his brother play the young Indiana Jones, although he would be later dismayed to find out that River turned down the chance to star in the TV series *The Young Indiana Jones Chronicles*. (When River died, Ford said, 'River Phoenix played my son and I came to love him like a son. I was proud to watch him grow into a man of such talent, integrity and passion.')

Firstly, he would work on *The Mosquito Coast*,

which would be shot in the English-speaking Central American country of Belize.

Weir said, 'We half heartedly surveyed Jamaica, and made queries about Costa Rica, Guatemala, Mexico and Hawaii, but Belize stood out.

'We found every location we needed, mountains, ocean, jungle, amazon-like rivers – all within a one-hour radius of Belize City. Belize also offered the advantages of an English language country reasonably close to the US, where the currency and political situation were both stable.'

While Ford stayed at a hotel nearby, River, his dad (who was on chaperone duties) and some of the cast and crew resided in the jungle.

Soon, the Phoenix family's true origins began to come to light – mainly from the studio, keen to highlight those similarities. Previously, River's colourful childhood had been brushed over, with many biographies listing him as being raised in California. Now they saw the chance to reveal his unusual upbringing. When asked if he felt close to the character in the film, River said, '*The Mosquito Coast* tells you to be true to someone you love. I knew that character so well because I was that character. I knew his whole past.'

While he and his father would spend time snorkelling,

or having adventures in the jungle – others noted that there was definite tension.

Talking about suggestions that John Phoenix wasn't happy about the drama, Weir opined that it was more than just John being unhappy with the film's source material, saying, 'When a young son suddenly becomes the key breadwinner of a family, an incredible amount of rearranging of things in the family hierarchy takes place, and sometimes a tension develops, particularly with the father. I do not know if that was true of John Phoenix, but River wanted to compensate. He did not want to spoil the family's closeness: John was in Belize with his son as the legally required chaperone, and seemed to be uneasy with the role his son was playing in *The Mosquito Coast*.

'Once, when John wanted to go off with his son to play the guitar, River refused, saying that he had to be responsible to the film and the others working on it. It's an example of the son growing beyond his childhood, seeking his own independence, and forming his own beliefs out of both opposition to an emulation of his father's creed, and gaining his own voice as creator of his own history.'

It was suggested that John could see his son growing away from him and his ideals, and that he tried to persuade him to take a trip to Guatemala during filming, but again River refused, reportedly telling him, 'I have to learn my lines and I have a responsibility to be on set and be rested.'

After *The Mosquito Coast* it was essential that River chose his future parts carefully. If he wanted to have longevity he had to show a wide range of talents.

Deciding that he would like to make a comedy, but one with a difference, he decided to plump for *A Night in the Life of Jimmy Reardon*, which was based on the book by William Richert, also the film's director.

Despite his father's warning not to make the movie because the character was something of a rogue (he couldn't believe his son was playing a selfish and an arrogant individual), River, Iris Burton and Arlyn agreed that it would show more depth to his range, and that he should definitely do the movie.

He would say about the role, 'He gets carried away by his dreams, which he wants to make happen in a day and a half. It's not the stereotypical coming-of-age film, because it's all seen through Jimmy's poetic point of view, and it does not really have a happy conclusion – nor should it. Jimmy ends up with nothing and nobody.

'He took a wrong turn somewhere along the line and I wouldn't want to be like him. Still, his intentions are beautiful. He wants to go to Hawaii and live in Paradise.

Everybody wants that. I created an outline of Jimmy's whole past so his actions would be understandable. Jimmy is more manipulative than I am, and bolder with women. Actually, this is the first movie in which I've done any kind of love scene, or comedy. I almost feel guilty getting paid.'

However, the film is said to have been re-cut and re-shot at the studio's behest into more of a sex romp than a coming-of-age drama – something that horrified River, who eventually moaned, 'I don't agree with that kind of film. *Jimmy Reardon* was one big mistake. I was very naïve and I didn't know that I was misusing my talents in a major way. I was exploiting something special.'

He added, 'It didn't turn out the way I thought it would. I'm not even sure I was the right person for the role. For it to work, I think you want to see someone a little bit more masculine, like Tom Cruise. He'd have done it much better than me.' His next role saw him play a much more clean-cut individual in *Nikita* – perhaps as a result of his dad's displeasure, which was growing each and every day.

Jimmy Reardon was the first film during which River wouldn't have his parents around on the set. They were in Florida looking after Leaf and Summer on the set of *Russkies*. His grandfather from Arlyn's side chaperoned him in any case – with the film's director remembering, 'River's grandfather did watch after him. I remember one time he said it was too cold outside and insisted I give River a coat.'

River's newfound independence reportedly saw him misbehave and get into drunken high jinks – but his co-star Louanne Sirota is quoted as saying, 'I don't remember River being out of control. We were good kids. He showed up on the set, he did what he was supposed to do, and was concerned about the role. He was very professional, treated everyone very well, and whatever time he had, he spent with his family and with us.

'The most out-of-control thing we ever did was order beer through room service when we were underage, and that was cool. He said, "Get on the phone, act all older and sexy, and say you want a six pack of Corona." So, I got on the phone and said, "Hi, this is so-and-so in room so-and-so. We'd like to get six Coronas." They brought up a bucket of Coronas and a bucket of ice. And here we are, sixteen years old, and we thought, "Man, we're gonna party." We had six beers. And to us that was cool. That is not out of control. That sounds normal, almost boring.'

The rebellion was also evident on *The Mosquito Coast*, which saw Phoenix distance himself from the vegan lifestyle. As well as drinking cans of coke, Weir revealed, 'he'd stuff himself with a Mars Bar.'

To satisfy his father's concerns, a compromise was reached.

The family would move into the swampland of Florida. The children could still work, but their daily life would be outside of LA. It was a compromise that seemed to please everyone. For John, it meant that he was minimising the perceived corruption his children were being exposed to, and his brood could have the 'normal' life they never had.

A large home outside Gainesville was their first port of call, before they would eventually find a ranch with a 20-acre estate. Their tutor Dirk Drake, who lived there for a few days a week, said, 'Their education was on the streets of the world. These kids had PhDs before they were ten. I knew how special these kids were because they had been raised with such special ideals. John and Arlyn [or Heart, as she now wanted to be called] had a mistrust of formal education. I think that was because of their own bad experience with public education as kids.'

River said about the move, 'It feels so good to be home. It feels good to settle down and live in a family and know what it really is like. I never wanted the wealthy fantasies of limousines or the pride of arriving at a school in nice clothes. I wanted money so we could buy a great piece of land and be self-contained. That impresses me, that really feels good. It feels likes something's been accomplished.'

He would add, 'People used to make fun of my family because we were so poor! But, I just knew that it wouldn't always be that way, that some day we'd be just fine.'

After he'd finished filming on *Russkies*, it would be another two years before Leaf was seen again on the big screen.

Before that there were appearances in TV movie *Secret Witness*, and guest appearances in *Still the Beaver* and *Superboy* – which saw him take centre stage in the episode, playing an insecure but potentially genius-like young boy, who inadvertently sets off a chain of events leading to a potential submarine missile attack. Again, he played an outsider, a soon-to-be recurring persona on screen, and he played it well. His bulging eyes and floppy hair created a rumpled, put-upon teenager who was trying to attract the beautiful girls while being bullied by a group of guys.

One of the show's stars, Stacy Haiduk, remembers being excited that the brother of teen heart-throb River Phoenix was going to be in an episode. 'I remember

Leaf coming in and he was River Phoenix's brother. I wasn't in that episode very much. I do recall he got to take a little flight in the suit,' she said.

A huge superhero fan, the young Phoenix was no doubt delighted to star in the show, which ran for four years. The episode features Joaquin in both the Superboy guise (a fantasy sequence) and then flying through the air with the actual superhero later on in the episode.

He would also be cast in the movie *Parenthood*, which this time saw him take on the role of a sullen teenager. It was easily his most impressive screen role to date, with the bulk of his work dialogue free. It would have been easy for audiences to dislike the troubled youngster as he sulks and slams doors wherever he goes, but in Joaquin's young hands he became a visibly troubled and sensitive kid rather than merely brattish.

Arguably, the most moving scene in the comedy drama comes when a young Leaf decides he wants to stay with his father instead of his mother. Keen not to upset his mother any more than necessary, he coyly but firmly tells her of his wishes, before phoning his dad to tell him of his plans. You never hear the other side of his conversation, but it's clear that he wants his dad more than his father wants him. The scene where he looks back at his mother, eyes filled with tears but body flinching into defence mode when his mother rushes over to comfort him, is a bravura moment for the young actor – although it must help anyone learning his trade to be acting alongside the always excellent Dianne Wiest.

The 1989 film focused on a multi-generational family and looked at the highs and lows of parenting. Apart from Wiest, his other main co-stars in his scenes were Keanu Reeves and Martha Plimpton – River's girlfriend and future *My Own Private Idaho* co-star. It also starred some of the best comedy talent of the eighties, including Steve Martin and Rick Moranis. The idea for the film came from Howard's experiences in dealing with his four children.

'At the beginning of a child's life, you have such high hopes and aspirations for your kids. Then they start going to school, talking back to you and exercising their own individuality. And when they get to the teenage years, they turn on you. Finally, when the kids get in their twenties and thirties, you think you're done being a parent. But then a crisis comes up and it doesn't matter if your child is five or twenty-five, you never stop being a parent.'

About the making of the movie, he added, 'Before we even shot a frame of film, I can say that I was very proud of this script. It's very funny while being very real and honest. There are ups and downs in the story and we don't back off on the dramatic themes.

'I've had two very good experiences with ensemble casts. First, as an actor in *American Graffiti* and then directing *Cocoon*. Both experiences taught me that the director has to balance and coordinate the acting styles. If not, you're left with pieces of a film, not one that is complete.'

While praising his cast, Howard reserved extra praise for Martin. 'Steve Martin is amazing at creating comedy. He finds the comedic root of any situation, even in mundane topics like child rearing. He understands better than anyone how comedy develops from character and situation.'

Producer Brian Grazer added, 'We had Steve Martin in mind from the beginning and we went after him. So if we didn't get him, the whole cast would have been different, since all the characters are related. The cast has to be believable in a story like this because any parent has experienced a part of this film.'

To make sure the ensemble cast worked, Howard made sure all the principal members, including Leaf, attended two weeks of rehearsals. And the rehearsals certainly worked, with the film becoming a box office and critical hit.

Variety stated, 'An ambitious, keenly observed, and

often very funny look at one of life's most daunting passages, *Parenthood*'s masterstroke is that it covers the range of the family experience, offering the points of view of everyone in an extended and wildly diverse middle-class family.'

Parenthood has now been turned into an hour-long US TV drama, starring *Gilmore Girls*' Lauren Graham, Peter Krause and Dax Shepard. It's the second attempt to try and replicate the film's success on the small screen. There was a half-hour version released in 1990, starring Leonardo DiCaprio, Thora Birch, Ed Begley Jr and David Arquette. It was a critical and commercial flop, however, and was cancelled after just 12 episodes.

Howard noted, 'Well, I came to believe that the half-hour model actually wasn't correct for the show. And so it would have either had to become a much broader show, with sort of quick hits and almost sketches on parenthood, or it needed to be what Jason [Katims, the creator of the new show] came to us to talk about, which was something that would really allow the characters to grow and evolve and worry less about framing up jokes and more about just reaching people in a way that resonated.

'In fact, the movie was always intended as a comedy but the simple storylines were dramatic and even dark. That was something that was impossible to work into the half-hour without just taking over the episode and then suddenly it wasn't a comedy. The growth of the family was kind of struggling there in that format. So we put it away and never considered bringing it back until Jason talked to us about it.'

Leaf was delighted with the film's success, but if he expected leading-man scripts to come his way he was to be disappointed. His former agent, and Iris Burton's right-hand man, Chris Snyder, said, 'There are a limited amount of projects out there when you are a child actor. You have to understand matching with parents weighs heavily into what roles that a child actor gets. It has nothing to do with how good you are. There are other factors, the matching the parents being one of them. Joaquin was never an actor of the cutesy Fred Savage, Macaulay Culkin type. But he was always a very good dramatic actor.

'Also, the location compromise that the Phoenixes were so happy to settle on was fine for actors like River, who had a place of sanctuary far away from Hollywood; for Leaf and the Burton Agency it would pose a problem. The move put a pin in his acting career because he was unavailable to audition.'

This was a time before the internet and phones with cameras, and with video equipment still expensive, even trying to film his auditions was a tricky process.

Snyder added, 'They didn't go to school the conventional way. They were home schooled. You needed to get a work permit, and getting a work permit became a problem because he wasn't in LA. He was in Florida, and he wasn't sixteen. And there were other little things like that. So we kind of waited until he was sixteen.'

Not that any of this bothered Leaf at that point – conceding that *Parenthood* ultimately 'ruined him' because he didn't think that he would find a better script. It didn't help that the scripts that were coming to him were just retreads of his *Parenthood* character. He was also reaching that difficult age for a child actor.

'I gave up when I was fourteen,' he said. 'I did a movie called *Parenthood*, which I liked a great deal. But the scripts that followed, I thought, were just dull. Y'know, white middle-class kids complaining about their problems. They just weren't detailed or fascinating enough for me, so about a year went by and, suddenly – no scripts came any more! Which, actually, was kind of fine by me.'

Snyder revealed, 'After *Parenthood* he kind of said, "I don't want to keep doing this." River was doing lots of work. His brother was a big deal and he was living in Florida. They had properties in Costa Rica or wherever. He just decided to take time off and not worry about it.'

His parents were beginning to drift apart, and John would travel with his son, before moving to Costa Rica to a retreat bought by River. It was something John had been desperate for, for years. He was hoping to persuade his children to come and live with him there, away from Hollywood. But only Leaf would join him on a temporary basis.

'I worked on a farm, actually, for quite some time. In Latin America,' Leaf recalled. 'I travelled through Mexico and Central America. I really liked the people there. They were spontaneous, friendly and unpretentious. I simply knew that I didn't want to make films any more at that time. The scripts that I was reading for ages fifteen through eighteen were just ridiculous. There's not a nice way to say it, the titles of them would just conjure up laughter. The year after *Parenthood*, I couldn't find anything that was of interest to me, so if you keep on saying "No" for a year, the offers stop and there's no work at all. That was fine with me.'

Joaquin would say in 1998, 'People always think it was strange and unstable but I just remember it being wonderful and exciting. When I was quite young, my family travelled across the States and I got to meet all sorts of people and experience difference things. Even when I was a kid I always felt comfortable travelling around in the van. That was just right for me. When I was about thirteen we settled down in a fairly small town, so I actually grew up in a small town. I never felt like we were different. I still don't.'

He travelled through Central America, desperate to grow as a person. It was around that time, thanks to River's coaxing, he realised that his original name was a good one, and decided to change his name back to Joaquin. It also didn't help that the name Leaf sounded a lot like the Spanish word for garlic.

'Here's the thing,' he said in 1997. 'There's ojo, ajo and hoja. That's "eye, garlic and leaf". So I was always messing it up with like, "What's your name?" "Garlic." "What's your name?" "Eye." They'd roll their eyes and laugh at me. It seemed like a good idea to change it back.'

The trip was something that Joaquin desperately needed to do, giving him freedom and the space to create his own identity. In his own words, 'I just grew up basically. I lost my virginity.'

Acting was still his goal, however. Despite reports that Joaquin took an enforced break, he was still being tested for roles.

Said Snyder, 'He did audition and flew to New York

to audition for the movies *The Ref*, *The Prince of Tides*, and *Billy Bathgate*. He screen tested in LA for *Scent of a Woman* and *This Boy's Life*. He was being considered for *Gilbert Grape* along with River. Again, getting parts is complicated and there are a great deal of factors that weigh into the decision.

'His acting and talent was and is still there. He just didn't get them. The age thing became a problem, but then it usually is for those actors. They normally cast eighteen-year-olds to play younger. He just wanted to come out for the good stuff, but there was no deliberate hiatus.'

Hearing of his brother's tentative attempts to head back to Hollywood, River was delighted. Snyder remembers River coming into his and Iris's office and saying that Joaquin was a better actor than him. The way River saw it, he knew Joaquin had the talent, and it wouldn't be long before Hollywood would too.

'They're totally different,' said Snyder. 'Joaquin was more intense. River made you feel comfortable. He was very accommodating, and he wanted to make you feel good.

'Joaquin kind of puts you on edge. Joaquin's a Scorpio, River's a Virgo. Different kinds of energies. Joaquin could be very seductive if he wanted to be however, very seductive indeed.'

There was the obvious hope from River that the two of them would share the screen once more, but it would be a forlorn one.

'River and I would talk about getting old, being in our fifties together, how it'd probably take us that long to get to work together,' Joaquin would say. 'There was something gorgeous about us being old together. River will be missed – period. I mean now, more than ever I wish I could talk to him.'

Despite his fame, and winning critical acclaim for *My Own Private Idaho*, River was having huge personal problems. The Iris Burton Agency received a phone call from the set of River's new movie, *The Thing Called Love* – warning them that they have to see his dailies [shots from the previous day's shoot]. It was clear something was wrong. Burton sat, smoke filling the air, and her heart sank as she watched the hugely promising and vibrant actor mumble and fidget through an hour of unusable footage.

Roger Ebert said in his review of the film, 'In Phoenix's first scene, it is obvious he's in trouble. The rest of the movie only confirms it, making *The Thing Called Love* a painful experience for anyone who remembers him in good health. He looks ill – thin, sallow, listless. His eyes are directed mostly at the ground. He cannot meet the camera, or the eyes of the other actors. It is sometimes difficult to understand his dialogue. Even worse, there is no energy in the dialogue, no conviction that he cares about what he is saying.'

It was clear something had to be done, so Burton and his mother Heart went down to Nashville to see if they could make the rest of the shoot uneventful. Their presence seemed to placate the older Phoenix sibling – who blamed his behaviour on the studio, sobbing in the arms of Burton and Snyder that it was their fault – and swearing that he wasn't on drugs.

Snyder had his obvious doubts and recalled an incident where the actor came to see him in his office, restless and out of sorts, and stared forlornly at the still of *Mosquito Coast* which sat proudly on Burton's bookcase. He still had his heart-throb looks and magnetic smile, but gone was the vulnerability and charismatic spark. He wanted to quit acting, telling Snyder, 'I don't even like this business any more. I don't know if I've ever liked it. I wasn't exactly given a choice.'

He talked about going to college, ruing the fact that he only played a high-school student on set, and had not actually done it for real.

He was set to make *Interview with the Vampire*. It was supposed to be a comeback role for him. His last few films had been box-office flops and critical nightmares. His movie *Silent Tongue*, which focused on a grieving widower who guards his dead wife's body, was deemed so weird that it couldn't attract a distributor. He had lost his edge. His agency knew it, but, more importantly, so did the studio bosses.

To get a role in a film that starred Tom Cruise and Brad Pitt was a huge olive branch, and a genuine chance to get River's career back on track. However, River wasn't interested in the role at first, turning down any scripts Burton sent him. Snyder would plead for him to read it, remarking how hard it was for them to get the part for him – adding that it was the most anticipated book adaptation since *Gone with the Wind* and that 'The studio aren't exactly bombarding you with projects right now.'

But while River didn't like the script he still felt he should have had one of the lead roles instead of that of the journalist, which is a somewhat minor but still important character. However, Snyder was able to convince Phoenix to take the part, on the basis that it would be a good career move – allowing him to get more of his independent films made.

His role in *Dark Blood*, which took the Burton Agency months to secure for him, was going well, much to the relief of Snyder, who was keenly aware that any troubles on the film would likely see him replaced on *Interview with the Vampire* – since *Dark*

Blood was being produced by *Interview with the Vampire*'s director Neil Jordan.

However, over a month into production and it was going well – the dailies looked great and it was passing without incident.

That was until the Iris Burton Agency received a frantic phone call. While working on *Dark Blood*, River had worked himself up into a state about a scene with a dead snake. Despite assurances that the snake died of natural causes, he worked himself to such a panic that he began screaming down the phone to the agency, accusing the film's bosses of being murderers. Not even getting a death certificate faxed was enough to placate him. Once again, Iris was called in to calm Phoenix down, and had to go to Salt Lake City.

It wasn't until soon after that it began to dawn on them that Phoenix could be indulging in Hollywood's trendiest drug, heroin.

Ethan Hawke is quoted as saying, 'Martha Plimpton was his first real girlfriend. Martha's wonderful and extremely smart, but it wouldn't be easy to have her as your first girlfriend. She doesn't buy any bullshit. In a way, that must have been good, because Martha would never tolerate drug abuse. But River and Martha didn't last.'

Joaquin said, 'The night he died we were together and he was just playing the guitar. He wanted to show me a new song, wanted to just go home and hang out, play the guitar. I was the one who wanted to go out and he just came because he was making sure I was taken care of.'

It was the evening of 30 October 1993. River had come to visit his older brother with his sister Rain.

A group of them, including River's girlfriend Samantha Mathis, headed out that night, starting off with a Halloween party in Hollywood Hills. They then headed to Johnny Depp's infamous club The Viper Room. As soon as they got in, they were escorted to the VIP area, where various hangers-on would scream furiously at a glance from River, who was easily recognisable despite his cropped jet-black hairstyle, done for a movie part. Depp was there that night (but he was in his own small VIP area downstairs), as was Red Hot Chili Peppers' guitarist John Frusciante and bass player Flea – who warmly greeted River when he saw him.

What happened next is up in the air. Some paint a night of drunken and drug-fuelled debauchery, while others suggest River was only there, guitar in tow, to play some songs with Johnny and Flea. The drugs that he took were a fatal experiment, or a regular occurrence with a tragic ending, depending on who you hear it from.

Eyewitness accounts have become Chinese-whispered over the years, and stories have been embellished. The only truth is that River took a deadly cocktail of heroin and cocaine in the toilets – famously known as a 'speedball'.

As soon as he took it, River knew something was wrong. He would firstly be ignored, and handed valium to calm him down. He washed his face with cold water again and again. He tried to walk back to the booth, unsteadily, falling down at Joaquin's feet. His head started spinning, and he gasped to anyone who would listen that something was wrong. He suddenly threw up all over himself and anyone who was close by. Still nothing was done, but eventually he was led outside to get some air. The door flew open, the wind brushed his face and River promptly fell, face first, onto the hard gravel.

It was assumed it was down to just too much of whatever he'd taken that night, drink or drugs. People milled around, unsure whether to laugh or be concerned. There was an agonising wait until they realised that something was indeed very wrong. River began having convulsions, his sister threw herself on him and a tearful Joaquin rushed to the nearest pay phone and frantically called 911.

The result of that phone call is only a google search

away, with your choice of a transcript or the actual audio recording needing only a click of your finger, after it was unforgivably leaked to the press. There's no need to repeat it here, only to say that it was the sort of anguished response you would hear from a brother who knew something was desperately wrong but clinging desperately on to the operator's comforting, but ultimately hollow, words.

The ambulance would eventually come, to find one of Hollywood's brightest stars lying on the pavement surrounded by a group of people, including a photographer. He was there to grab a picture of the celebs that always found their way to The Viper Lounge. It was famous for its rock-and-roll energy, and the coolest place to go if you wanted to be seen as having a dangerous rock edge.

From then on, it would only be synonymous for one thing – the death of 23-year-old actor River Phoenix.

'It's tragic, because part of me wants to open up. I mean, there are things that I'd love to clear up. But at the same time, the more I state that publicly, that can be taken, used and distorted, the more I add to my family's grief and my own grief,' said Joaquin.

'I'm still…it's very difficult to talk about it because when you lose something, someone, it's such a great loss, you try and hold onto anything that you have, and memories that you have, and what was so difficult and what scarred me for a long time was when those memories were robbed from me. I wasn't allowed to experience them on my own time. Other people took advantage of their access to me, and suddenly my memories were distorted and changed. So it's very difficult, it's hard for me to talk about it now. When you lose someone, you need to go through a really long period to try and understand what's happened and to feel that loss in your own way. It's more difficult if it's a public death because it's going to take you that much longer to try and understand what's happened.'

CHAPTER FOUR

THE MOURNING
AFTER

The death of River Phoenix was announced to a
stunned world the following morning.

Associated Press ran with: 'River Phoenix, whose
natural intensity as a teenage actor in the 1986 film
Stand By Me launched his career, collapsed outside a
nightclub early yesterday and died. He was twenty-three.
Friends reported that Phoenix was "acting strange" as
he left the Viper Room in West Hollywood about 1am
said sheriff's deputy Diane Hecht. She didn't elaborate.
Paramedics were called when the actor collapsed, and he
was rushed to Cedar-Sinai Medical Center.'

Anyone looking for a reason to explain Joaquin's
seeming distrust of the media even now, only has to

look at the grisly press aftermath; he had a first-hand look at the ugly side of Hollywood and the media, with pictures being leaked of River in his casket, and his anguished 911 call made public.

'This 911 call was sent into the radio and television. It was terrible. They photographed him in his coffin. And these hysterical girls who were at the funeral almost fell into the grave. Repulsive. It was a long time before I overcame this shock,' he said.

Nevertheless, Joaquin would wryly admit that it would have been far worse if he had died now: 'When my brother passed it was toward the end of an era. If it had happened much later, it would have been on a lot of fucking blogs.

'The amount of information flying back and forth now has just gone beyond comprehension...In some ways it's hard to swallow. It makes you feel sick about yourself and about human beings. You look at yourself and say, "When have I exploited others and been voyeuristic?" The thing we should be discussing in the news, what the media should be going after in a heartless way, isn't the family of somebody who has passed away, but instead – oh, I don't know – how about a president who's lying?

'That's not to say my brother's life didn't have value, but it certainly did not deserve to be covered more than world politics and other important issues, particularly when death happens every day to millions of people all over the world and we don't seem to give a fuck about that.'

Of that night he also said, 'My brother's death has been spread across the world. The press has been heartless. It's entertainment to them. I had reporters in my face asking questions like, "How come you were so polite when you called 911?" Heartless bastards! How do they even begin to know how I felt that night?

'The tabloids sent planes and helicopters over our house the morning after my brother died. Can you imagine my mother seeing cover after cover of my dead brother's face? It was a terrible thing that was made much, much, much more difficult by the frenzy. Honestly, I don't know how you make it through these things. I still have a lot of hate and anger and pain.'

In another interview, he simply stated, 'People are heartless. What can you do? Motherfuckers are cold.'

Burton stayed in her bedroom for days, only coming out to get some food. Her phone was unplugged and her nose wouldn't stop bleeding. Her office rang constantly, letters filled the room and on one occasion one deranged fan insisted that River was reborn in his body and he wanted Iris to keep representing the late actor through him.

Johnny Depp wanted to donate the door of The Viper Room, which was now daubed with messages from well-wishers. Snyder said he should contact the family.

Depp said shortly afterwards, 'We had met. We weren't close friends, and on a professional level, I respected him as an actor. I mean, there was a specific road he was on that I respected as an actor...and it's really unfortunate and a waste. I feel terrible for his family. And, I felt angry at the way that the media handled it. And, that's the tabloid press and the legitimate press. A lot of the legitimate press, I thought, really merged with the tabloids on this thing and exploited the situation, and I thought it was disrespectful and unfortunate that his family and friends had to experience that 911 call, you know. And, I don't know his family, but I understand they're a very close, strong family. I'm sympathetic.'

A family service was held in Florida, and was overseen by an old family friend – Father Wood. Around 60 people, comprising family members and his closest friends, attended.

Heart, meanwhile, told Wood that her 'main concern right now was helping the other children through this.'

They were all devoted to River, worshipful, and it was terrible for them that she couldn't really show how she felt.

A Hollywood ceremonial service was held at Paramount Studios – the same place where Burton and Snyder had watched River's lethargic performance in *The Thing Called Love*. It was the biggest draw in Hollywood – anyone who was anyone in the film industry attended. According to Snyder, more of them were there to be seen rather than to pay their respects. He would claim that over 100 people would be milling outside the theatre, smoking and talking shop – more concerned about who was being recast in River's character in *Interview with the Vampire*.

His death brought out both the worst and the desperate in Hollywood. The genuine well-wishers who had come to pay their respects with no ulterior motives were in the minority. Seen and being heard is as essential as breathing in LA – whether it was a fancy brunch, lavish premiere or, in this case, a memorial service for an actor who many were beginning to believe had passed his sell-by date as a box office draw before his death.

However, if you throw enough media attention at an event they will come.

And come they did.

It was an incident-packed service, which started with *A Night in the Life of Jimmy Reardon's* Bill Richert wanting to play a tape recording River had left a year before – something that Burton was aghast at. Some of the famous speakers included Dame Helen Mirren, Sidney Poitier and Rob Reiner – the latter recounting a story about River losing his virginity on the set of *Stand By Me*, while his *Running on Empty* screen mom Christine Lahti said that he was so sexy she didn't know whether to mother him or date him.

There were also letters read out from those who would have been his *Interview with the Vampire* co-stars, Brad Pitt and Tom Cruise. Burton would speak – saying, 'This innocent little bird got his wings clipped in the most evil city in the world.'

His mother Heart said, 'We believed we could use the mass media to help change the world and that River would be our missionary. I sensed from the beginning, as my labour extended to three-and-a-half days, that River didn't want to be in this world. I woke up two days after his death, understanding for the first time why the dawn is called morning and suddenly had a vision of how God had tried to convince River to be born one more time. River told God, I'd rather stay up here with you. So they bargained, God was persuasive, and River offered to go for five years, and then ten and finally agreed to visit Earth, but only for twenty-three years. River is still with me.

'Whenever the wind blows, I see River, when the sun shines I see River, when I look in someone's eyes and see a connection, I see River. To have death transformed into another way to look at life is his huge gift.'

Snyder commented on the speech, saying, 'Whereas Iris had been overwhelmed with grief, Heart read her speech without much emotion.'

Jane Campion admitted she didn't know River but she had just lost her ten-year-old son and wanted to come to understand why these things happen. The ceremony just kept getting stranger and stranger, with Peter Bogdanovich's wife standing up and saying, 'Peter and I adopted this stray cat that came around the house every day. We know my sister Dorothy is reincarnated in that cat...'

The tone would then turn decidedly awkward when director John Boorman mentioned the giant elephant in the room. He said, 'Is there anybody here who can tell us why River took all those drugs.'

Boorman's comments shocked the room, with Heart particularly mortified that anyone would dare bring that up now. To her, the drug-taking allegations were only reserved for Hollywood tittle-tattle. To them, the blame was on an unforgiving industry burdening a forgiving soul. At least that's how she and her husband felt, with River's death bitterly vindicating what John had feared most.

River had seen him in Costa Rica shortly before his death and they had talked about getting him out of Hollywood. He looked at his dad, hugely content with life, enjoying running his Costa Rican vegan restaurant – his only disappointment being that his children weren't there to help him with it. 'Things were buzzing. The idea was for them to spend more time here, helping with cooking, making music, writing, harvesting the organic fruit and living off the land like we used to,' John had said.

In 1993, John added, 'I could see Hollywood eating him up, bleeding him dry. I told him I wanted him out of the movies. I had been urging him to quit for some time. I had seen too many brilliant kids go down and I realised he couldn't buck the system. I thought it was time for him to stop.'

According to various sources, River ended their visit promising he would quit Hollywood once work on *Dark Blood* and *Interview with the Vampire* was finished.

John said, 'I'll always remember, he told me, "I'll see you after this movie, Dad." Well he did. Only he was in a box. Our original idea was for him to make enough movies for us to be financially secure – milk the system, if you want – then stop. We had made enough money to keep all those closest to us ... in-laws outlaws, friends, environment groups, whatever, and I wanted us all to get out.

'Still, the pressure was there to keep going, make more. Hollywood is the great Babylon. They care for money and nothing else. It's an evil, bad place. But these people were something else. It started to take him over. So many assholes cater for your every need. There were times when people should have said, "No, River. Actually, it's late. I'm tired, and so are you."'

John would add, 'We all feel guilt, everyone who knew River. Not a day goes by when I don't think long and hard about River's death and ask myself why.'

Heart left the memorial in protest following Boorman's comments, along with Summer and Liberty. Boorman would later explain his remarks: 'His mother said that she'd been in labour with River for forty-eight hours, and that she was convinced he hadn't really wanted to be born. She thought he had struck some sort of deal so that he wouldn't have to stay very long on this earth. People were invited to say things, and I had that feeling that people get at Quaker meetings, where they suddenly start to shake. So I got up and said, "Why did he have to take all those drugs?"

'People shouted and screamed at me – they were horrified I could ask that question. But it seemed to me that it had been hanging in the air. His girlfriend stood up and said that she thought he could feel people's pain: the pain of the world. And he had to find a way to dull that pain. He simply couldn't deal with it.'

He added, 'I met with River a few times. He was streetwise, but at the same time there was this fragility about him. You felt that somehow he had to be protected. Many people felt that he was vulnerable and open.'

Interview with the Vampire producer Stephen Woolley predicted, 'I suspect he would have gone on to play harder, more interesting characters. Robert Downey Jr is exactly the kind of guy that River would have become had he lived. There's a comparison there in the conflict between what pays the rent and what challenges you creatively, and also, I think, in the way they were both hung out to dry. I was quite surprised at the end when it became apparent that there was no one looking after River. Nobody could, he was a grown man, of course, but in another sense he was still a kid. The way he died was by visiting little sections of friends, none of whom were aware of the other, getting a little bit of this, a little bit of that. He was very cleverly playing everyone. He just had no one in his life who was strong enough to say, "What are you doing now, where are you going?"'

On 24 November, Heart penned an article in the *LA Times*, celebrating her son's life:

'I think people want to know if River ran his course or if he was taken from the world prematurely.

'River was my first born. He introduced me to motherhood and has been the strongest influence on my life. I feel blessed to have been the woman who held him deep within my being as he grew from a tiny seed. I birthed him at home, suckled him to a chubby two-year-old and then held him in love and awe until his safe passage on Oct. 31.

'It was incredible to watch River grow. From the beginning, he was a soul filled with passion and a sense of service for others. At a young age, he took on the responsibility of sharing the

wonderful gifts that were given him. He diligently taught himself guitar at four, sang on the streets from Venezuela to Westwood, Calif., and wrote music and lyrics, seeking to open hearts in a new way.

'*Many of you have been able to experience his openness, gentleness, beauty and vulnerability on the screen. He chose characters that reached inside the souls of the audience, awakening long-forgotten feelings. With River's passing, people the world over have been touched by the loss and once again their deep feelings have surfaced.*

'*The coroner's report states that drugs were the cause of death. His friends, co-workers and the rest of our family know that River was not a regular drug user. He lived at home in Florida with us and was almost never a part of the "club scene" in Los Angeles. He had just arrived in LA from the pristine beauty and quietness of Utah where he was filming for six weeks. We feel that the excitement and energy of the Halloween nightclub and party scene were way beyond his usual experience and control. How many other beautiful young souls, who remain anonymous to us, have died by using drugs recreationally? It is my prayer that River's leaving in this way will focus the attention of the world on how painfully the spirits of his generation are being worn down.*

'They are growing up with polluted air, toxic earth and food, and undrinkable water. We are destroying our forests, the ozone layer is being depleted, and AIDS and other diseases are epidemic. The world is a very confusing place for most young people and we need to address that. Drug abuse is a symptom of an unfeeling, materialistic, success-oriented world where the feelings and creativity of young people are not seen as important. Drugs, including alcohol, are used to soften the pain of feeling separated from ourselves, each other and love. We can't just say "Just Say No" – it's ridiculous we need to offer our children something they can say "Yes" to.

She added, 'River made such a big impression during his life on Earth. He found his voice and found his place. And even River, who had the whole world at his fingertips to listen, felt deep frustration that no one heard. What is it going to take? Chernobyl wasn't enough. Exxon Valdez wasn't enough. A bloody war over oil wasn't enough. If River's passing opens our global heart, then I say, thanks dear, beloved son, for yet another gift to all of us.'

Joaquin's grief was palpable, and he was beyond numb. Director Peter Bogdanovich recalled the first time he met Joaquin, 'He was having a cigarette in the living room. We hadn't met before, but Joaquin said that River had spoken well of me. As he tried to speak of his brother, Joaquin broke down. Recalling the terrible moments, he began sobbing and couldn't go on. I embraced him. He held on to me and kept crying.'

At River's Florida memorial, Father Wood said, 'I was concerned for Joaquin. He'd grown up, but I still remembered him as a little kid. Somehow, my being there provided a necessary release for him. He cried in my arms for a long time. He just seemed like he had a whole lot pent up. Maybe he'd cried already. Maybe it was just one more time. I don't want to claim any special connection with him, but at that moment we connected enormously. He gave me a very firm and extended *abrazo* [hug]. I think he really needed it. And I will always remember it'

His *SpaceCamp* director Harry Winer, recalling the moment River had stepped in to save the day with some tender brotherly advice during filming, opined,

'When you think about the bond he clearly had with his brother and losing him at a young age, what sort of impact that had on him.'

Unfortunately, his grieving wasn't helped by the media postmortem, which would see people queuing up to offer their 'insight'.

Joaquin's guilt felt heavier than the grief. He claims he was the one who persuaded River to head out that night, with River preferring to stay at home and play guitar. Suggestions that he didn't want to upset River about his drug use because he was the Phoenixes money train are of course nonsense. It's true that there was a large dependence on River's income, but if anything his career was plummeting fast precisely because of the possible drug problems. The reason why any of his family could not reason with him if they so wished to is the same reason no one can with an addict – especially one who was put on a pedestal as River had been by his parents. As stated before, however, there is no evidence of any resentment from Joaquin about River, but there was an almost worshipful feeling to him.

But the focus was now on Joaquin.

Rain would call him 'My cool gauge. If he thinks something's cool, then I feel good about it.'

He would say about his new role with his sister a

few years later, 'I'm trying to be there for them. I look back on movies I didn't get and how it crushed me. I learned when I was young not to expect too much.'

He also said in another interview, 'I had a really wonderful upbringing. We were a tight family. It was wonderful to grow up with so many siblings. We were all just a year or two apart, and we were always so supportive of each other. I learned everything from my older brother and sister and taught it to my younger sisters.

'We used to go to Westwood at Christmas and sing on the streets. We managed to get enough money to go to JC Penny and my parents found these yellow tank tops and gold shorts but we could only afford two of the gold shorts, so River and Rain got them. My dad helped us with dance moves, they were really primitive and synchronised. Summer was so cute, she didn't even know the words.'

Talking once more about River, he added, 'I've come nearer acceptance – I wouldn't say understanding, because it's something I'll never understand – but just an acceptance of River's death.'

His friends had suggested he try to get back into acting to take his mind off things. He wasn't sure, but he still agreed to go for roles.

His future girlfriend Liv Tyler said, 'He's said to me he feels so much happier when he's working. He's got so much in his little head all the time; he's got so many ideas.'

Phoenix said, 'I just became interested in the work again. I guess I'd just grown as an individual and a human, and felt that there were things I wanted to express. Auditioning is a whole different style of acting. So I'd go in and read for stuff like *Lassie Comes Home* – dog and whale movies. I thought, "God, this is going nowhere." Then I read *To Die For.*'

Initially he'd left the script for *To Die For* (1995) unread in his home for months, reasoning, 'I just wasn't interested. I just have this tendency to expect the worst from a story. You know, I always see really bad acting, for some reason.'

But after reading it, he exclaimed, 'Whoa, this is what I've been missing these last few years.' He became obsessed with the role, reading it, predicting how the character of Jimmy would react throughout the film, and getting most of it right. He instinctively knew where the character was, and became as excited as he ever has been about a role.

A short film called *Walking the Dog* aside, which he filmed in 1991 (with the director hailing his Steve

McQueen-type persona), this would be Joaquin's first film role since 1989.

It would be Phoenix's first film since his brother's death. However, the film he would choose would be one with a director that is forever entwined with River. *My Own Private Idaho* is arguably River's most iconic film, and now Joaquin's potential breakthrough role was in the hands of director Gus Van Sant.

In an interview with *The Face* magazine, Van Sant recalled, 'I think that getting together with me to work on the film was difficult at first because I automatically reminded him of River. He understandably doesn't like to be reminded of him. He still usually says "My brother" instead of "River" and rarely brings him up. He likes to hear stories about him, though, and listens when I talk about what he used to do and say. I never ask questions about him. It's just something you don't bring up.'

The film would be a dark comic-drama based on the novel by Joyce Maynard, which was itself based on a real-life incident that took place in 1990, when a New Hampshire man was shot to death by a 16-year-old kid. It transpired that the man's wife had seduced a teenager and threatened to break off their sexual relationship if he did not end the life of her husband.

It was a sensational story, and one that would be covered in length by the US media, resulting in both a TV movie and a fictionalised take on the events – the latter winding up in the hands of producer Laura Ziskin, who would promptly ask Van Sant to direct the picture.

Van Sant had had an eclectic career. He had risen to fame after shooting the movie *Drugstore Cowboy*, and would go on to make such wonderful pieces of work as *My Own Private Idaho* and *Good Will Hunting*, would turn down eventual hit films like *Sleeping with the Enemy* and *Cape Fear* and would famously direct a pretty much derided shot-for-shot remake of Alfred Hitchcock's *Psycho*.

Ziskin said, 'Gus is a real artist. He has a fabulous eye and, I say this in the best sense, an idiosyncratic way of shooting and a somewhat idiosyncratic design sense that is very strong, defined and clear. His style and Henry's writing talents seemed like a good mix for the project.'

Writer Buck Henry said, 'Since one of the central themes of the book is the siren call of public media and its effect on the participant and the viewer, how could I make that part of the structure? So I came around to the idea that all of these people are telling these stories for a reason other than just telling the stories. I don't like voice-overs. I think, with a few exceptions, when movies have voice-overs it's because the filmmaker has failed to find a dramatic course to take that covers the information. But a straight voice-over is the same thing as a straight talk to camera, it's a fall back position. Anyway, in a flash of either inspiration or obviousness, I thought, "Oh, yes, of course. They're all entertaining on different media".'

Speaking of the role of the wife, Suzanne, he said, 'The problem, then, was finding a reason for Suzanne to talk to the camera, since I knew she was dead. That's why I devised her taping her story, which in itself becomes part of the plot.'

Van Sant's last film, *Even Cowgirls Get the Blues*, which starred Rain, had been a flop – with *New York Post* calling it so 'breathtakingly bad that it actually leaves the viewer in a state of numbed disbelief.'

But Van Sant quipped, 'Fortunately, I was already shooting *To Die For* when *Cowgirls* came out. If you're looking for work when a movie gets shot down, you're in trouble ... I did have a moment of panic on the set the morning the *Cowgirls*' reviews came. I'd never received such public ridicule, so I went to work that day convinced that no one would listen to me. I wondered, "Are the actors going to come to work? Is the crew going to forget to load the film?"'

Meg Ryan was originally earmarked for the star part, but when she left, a rising Australian actress saw a role perfect for her. She rang up the director, announcing, 'I am destined to play Suzanne.' It was an ambitious move, drawing comparisons with the film's main character. Names like Jodie Foster, Bridget Fonda, Uma Thurman and Michelle Pfeiffer were all linked to the role. But Nicole Kidman was desperate to play the part, even phoning the director at his house.

Gus Van Sant commented, 'In a way, it's just something you would say. But I took it a different way, like she really was destined to play the role. When she showed up, she was very prepared and worked very hard on her own to develop the character.

'I don't know why she [Meg Ryan] changed her mind, but perhaps the character was too dark for her. The character is annoying at some points and you might feel the audience is going to hate her.'

But Van Sant had a good feeling about the 27-year-old Kidman and, impressed by her performance in the recent thriller *Malice*, offered her the role on the spot – a generally rare thing for a Hollywood movie, particularly to someone who flitted between roles in popcorn junk like *Days of Thunder* and *Batman Forever* and thrillers like *Malice* and *Dead Calm*.

She was of course married to Tom Cruise – ironically, Kidman's character in the novel says that if she ever gets played by an actress in a film about her life she wants whoever it is to be married to Tom Cruise. Van Sant would claim that he had no idea who she was married to.

The film focuses on a beautiful female whose ruthless ambition to be a famous news anchorwoman far outstrips her actual talents. To achieve her dream she begins by marrying a local man (Matt Dillon) with Mafia connections, and then begins her attempts to become famous. A spanner is thrown in the works when Dillon's character Larry tries to persuade her to give up her job in a bid to raise a family. Horrified, she forms a plot to kill him – namely by attempting to seduce Joaquin Phoenix's student, Jimmy. It was a classic film-noir plot but, like another future Phoenix film, *Clay Pigeons*, it would be done with a darkly comic twist – hard-boiled with humour.

Despite loving the script, Joaquin wasn't necessarily a cert for the part. He faced a battle with none other than Matt Damon.

'Matt looked like the football quarterback, not the emancipated kid from the other side of the tracks,' recalled Gus. 'Matt was an extremely adept actor, very quick, and he really wanted the part. Probably more so than anybody I interviewed. Matt tried hard to get it to the point where – he was twenty three – and I said, "You're just a little too old," and he said, "No, no. I can act younger if you give me a couple of weeks." And he starved himself so he was really skinny and he somehow focused his eyes so he looked not as intelligent, and a little green, not as worldly, about six years less wordly. He really did look sixteen, and I said, "God, that's amazing." And I kind of forgot to say, "But you're too all-American."'

He was still in Van Sant's mind, however, and it essentially came to a toss-up between Damon and Phoenix.

Talking once about his casting process, Van Sant revealed, 'Beginning with my film *Mala Noche*, I took the pictures of the lead actors, so that when planning details of the shoot I could stare at the pictures and imagine the characters coming to life, and how they might visually relate to one another. As my films grew larger and when I decided to get more money to make them, I used the polaroids of the faces to do the initial casting.

'I sort of display them on the wall or use them almost like playing cards to figure out your cast. Play eight guys down and see, like, if they're working together.

Like, take one out and put one in like solitaire or something. I can do that endlessly. I can sit there and mix and match for days and days.'

He went on, 'As I look closely at the pictures, I am reminded about the power a single person carries around with them. Everyone is different, and yet they all look the same. They all embody huge potential for success or failure, for nervousness or calm, for sainthood or devilry, and have individually their proportionate share of both. They remind me of the moment the picture was taken, and how that moment is linked to their past, present and future.'

About his eventual choice, he said, 'It was really neck and neck. But Joaquin was the obvious favourite. I thought Matt was very good, although Joaquin was more of a name than Matt Damon.'

He would go on to say further, 'It was a tough story. His character kills somebody, and I didn't know if it was too freaky, if it was something he could handle. But he decided he wanted to do it. He thought the script was very funny. I didn't want the producer or casting director to think it was nepotism or something, so I let them say, "He's the best" first. I knew already that he was my first choice, but this was right after River died, and there was a question as to whether he wanted to act in anything.'

Phoenix was cast, and quickly decided on how to play the character. Seizing on certain key descriptions of the character, he decided to get hair extensions and go for a Billy Ray Cyrus look. Starring alongside Phoenix was Casey Affleck (brother of Ben, and recommended for the film by Damon), who would later to go on to marry and have two kids with Joaquin's sister, Summer.

She told the *Observer*, 'I don't recall that much [on how they met], actually, but he's got the story that I ran into him on the street when I was with my brother. And my brother was like (she adopts a Neanderthal teen male voice), "Uh, yeah, this is my sister..." and I was awestruck. And then for, I swear it was eight years, we hung around in the same circles, sometimes, but he was at school, and he was pretty mysterious: "Yeah, I'm in school all the time, I don't have time to come out, I don't smoke, I don't drink, I'm not partying." And he would just make fun of me all the time, like a big brother would.

'[Eight years later] My brother was staying at Casey's apartment in New York when Casey was out of town, and I joined him for a few days. Casey called and asked to speak to me. We talked for a time and I said: "You have a beautiful apartment." He said: "The only thing missing is you. Be there for me when I get back." So I stayed.'

As an adult on a film set for the first time, this was a weird experience for Phoenix – especially as he had a love scene with Kidman.

Joaquin would say, 'A director can have a lot of power, but you never feel that way around Gus. I think any authority can be intimidating. But with Gus it feels like you're working with a friend on a student film, and that you can do no wrong.'

Talking about their sex scene, the director said, 'A gay director who is directing a straight sex scene is removed, which helps. He can objectively see what the dynamics of the two characters are. But when you're making movies, it's like designing a building. If you're designing a room and you're gay, there are some things that will be affected – maybe the shape of room, the interior decoration. But when you're talking about just getting people through doors with the right kind of perspective, your sexuality doesn't necessary apply. And a sex scene is architecturally rendered by the filmmaker. The actual sexuality of the characters is the last thing you come in contact with.

'First of all, you're just trying to get across to the audience that two people are in bed. When you're learning to make movies, it's hard just to set up your first camera angle. You realise, oh, the audience doesn't know we're in a room if I shoot your face too close. You get into very basic graphic representation of things. Eventually you get to a state where you want the characters to be intimate. Their sexuality is the last thing to be manipulated.'

Despite his genuine talent, Joaquin suffered from huge insecurity. Filming a pivotal scene where Kidman's character finally manipulates Jimmy into agreeing to kill her husband saw a downbeat Phoenix turn down a request to join the rest of the crew and cast during downtime to watch episodes of British sitcom *Absolutely Fabulous*. Instead, he preferred to walk around the set alone, annoyed at himself for not getting the scene the way he wanted.

Van Sant would note that Phoenix was always 'trashing himself' – unlike his brother, who had had complete confidence in his acting talents. The director told *The Face*, 'It was the opposite of River. River would know when he did a scene well. If someone suggested that maybe he should have tried another approach, he'd debate it and say, "No, no, it was really good." You'd never say that to Joaquin or it would send him into a tailspin of self-criticism. In the end, both ended up doing good work, only one was confident, the other's not.'

To say the least. There have been endless reports of

Joaquin's self confidence ebbing away, whether it's a scene not provoking the response desired, or the most mundane of things like wondering whether an waitress's bad mood was brought on by him. (It happened in front a journalist in 1995, and her mood had nothing to do with him. Didn't stop him worrying about it constantly though.)

Snyder said, 'I've never met anyone with lower self-esteem than Joaquin.'

His future director, Oliver Stone, would comment, 'He runs a higher standard on himself than anyone else, but that's part of his background. He comes from that damaged reputation. Low self-esteem, that kind of thing. There's something very pure about him. There's no consciousness of cool at all.'

There were no such problems with Kidman.

Van Sant said, 'You can always do good work even if you're only half into it, but she put in extra time. She was obsessed with perfection, which is definitely in contrast with my personality. I got to Hollywood and I see these people waking up at 5.30 to read ten international papers, then have a power breakfast, read a script, have another breakfast, and then spend two hours on the phone to London. You have to be like that if you're going to be successful in Hollywood, and Nicole is that way.'

Talking about her character, Van Sant said, 'There are people like Nicole Kidman's character that I knew who wanted to escape from their environment and become something in the big world. What was special about their life living in a town where they knew everybody and people talked to them daily, was what the big city lacked.

'This character is really scary because you like her and she's the lead. Some actor's natural reaction in that situation is to say, "I know the audience is going to dislike me, but how do I get them to like me?" That's not the solution. You have to like to dislike the character.

'She's in almost every scene, so she had to have this kind of interpretive openness. I also think the wig that she wears helps a lot. She said it did. Even a slight disguise can bring out something unpredictable in someone.'

Van Sant would add, 'You are channelling everybody's energy – the cinematographer's, the actors', and trying to channel something to make the scene come alive. I think for me, it's mainly keeping everybody comfortable, very comfortable, where they can make a mistake and it's OK to try something new, or don't be afraid to goof because you can always roll again. And once everybody's really comfortable, the

119

different styles and the different experiences kind of equal out, and then people can have fun together. I like to do just a couple of takes if it's appropriate, depending on the actor.'

Joaquin's mother would appear frequently, watching rushes of the film with him at the end of the day, while Kidman marvelled at how close they were, watching the rushes with his head on her shoulder.

Tom Cruise did not appear on set – with Van Sant reasoning, 'She wouldn't do her best work with him in the room. It's a pretty major disruption on the set, like having the Beatles there. It was accepted that he wasn't going to attend, though he came on the set instantly when we were done. A lot of it has to do with his stature. He's too large a presence. It would affect me, it would affect everybody.'

While Nicole Kidman would be hailed as brilliant by critics, CNN reserved praised for Joaquin, saying, 'The most remarkable member of the cast is Joaquin Phoenix (brother to the late and lamented River). He's cast as one of a trio of grungy teens who Suzanne seduces into bumping off her hubby. Frankly, it's hard to tell how much Phoenix is acting here and how much he's just "being". In either case, his portrayal resonates – raw, in many ways, but achingly real. There's one point in the film when he passionately yet pitifully describes Suzanne as "clean". It's so sad. So stupid. Yet Phoenix makes the audience believe he means it with every fibre of his hormonally overwhelmed body and his none-too-functional brain.'

Newsweek would claim, 'It's a surprising movie from Van Sant. Gone is the wiggy lyricism of *Drugstore Cowboy* and *My Own Private Idaho*, replaced by a remarkably disciplined black-comic edge. The imprint of Henry's sardonic intelligence is obvious, but you can feel Van Sant's touch most strongly in the spooky pathos of Phoenix's odd and affecting performance – he's literally blurry with lust. In another director's hands, *To Die For*'s satirical venom could have turned sour and obvious.'

It was a performance that instantly forced the media to place Joaquin and his late brother in some sort of acting contest – which Phoenix is the better looking, who's the better actor. It would be something that would crop up time and time again during the nineties, and one he would address with a weary sigh. One journalist asked him if he had ever read a script and wished him and River could be in it – to which he responded, 'No, I don't really care about the movie we will never do together. I just wish we could still be brothers.'

His personal life seemed to be going as well as his

professional one – he was dating Acacia at the time. She was a green-eyed brunette, and Phoenix doted on her, calling her his best friend. They were a playful couple – constantly high-fiving and nuzzling each other affectionately. During their relationship he would hang out at her Chinatown apartment, where they spent late nights with their friends listening to music.

Sadly, fears of him being typecast after his breakthrough role were more than justified, however. He was shocked to find that the first film role offered to him after the film was released was a script for a movie of the week, which focused on a woman who seduced a young man, and asked him to kill her husband.

At the same time, the Burton Agency was losing its allure – going from 120 clients to around a dozen, the main ones being Kirsten Dunst and Joaquin. However, just like the experience he'd dealt with in *Parenthood*, as soon as he put in a great performance, he was once again typecast – with nothing but *To Die For* indentikits.

'I got offered a lot of stoned, stupid, vulnerable kid characters after *To Die For*. I just kept saying no, no, no and I guess they got the hint. I just want to be good.'

Joaquin hadn't worked in over 18 months – and Burton was having problems finding work for him, with the scripts that were coming through often strange or ones that he had done before. His agency advised him against doing the same roles – keenly aware that once typecast your career will stagnate

'It wasn't so much finding him roles,' Snyder said. 'He was being offered them, they were just all the same characters. That is just what happens in Hollywood. He would suddenly have twenty-five scripts that had him in the same role.

'There's a great actor called Jeremy Davis. He's been in *Saving Private Ryan* and lots of movies. The problem is he plays the same role in every movie. He actually got a movie that I wanted for Joaquin, *Spanking the Monkey*. (David O. Russell's hip 1994 American independent movie focuses on a young man and his incestuous relationship with his mother.)

'It was David O. Russell's first movie, and I loved that script. I gave it to Joaquin. He went for a meeting, put him on tape, they were interested but Jeremy got the role. It's funny because after that there were other roles we wanted for Joaquin but Jeremy got them, but they were the same role and Jeremy Davies now has a hard time getting work.'

Joaquin was being handed scripts, but he still wasn't sure about them. Snyder stumbled upon a horror script called *Scream*, immediately spotted the film's potential, and was desperate for Joaquin to go for it, but Iris wouldn't hear of it. 'This agency does not do horror films. Never have, never will. All that blood is disgusting.'

Snyder would read something, however, that blew him away – labelling it as one of those scripts that comes up every once in a while. It was called *Boogie Nights*, and it dealt with a young man's foray into the porn industry. According to Snyder, he sent the script without her permission, which angered her. And her mood wouldn't get any better when he relayed to her the plot of *Boogie Nights* – a drama centring on a young man who becomes a porn star, before falling into a world of drugs.

Burton couldn't believe her ears.

She was certainly into more mainstream fare. In the trailer of River's *The Thing Called Love* she would sit aghast as the Phoenix siblings watched a rough cut of Gus Van Sant's *Even Cowgirls Get the Blues*, which starred Rain, giving, what Snyder would call, one of her what-the-fuck-is-this looks. And, despite the acclaim, she was not exactly enamoured with Van Sant's *My Own Private Idaho* – calling it *My Own Private Jerkoff*, despite the fact that the film featured one of River's most iconic performances and Van Sant had give Joaquin's career a much needed jolt in *To Die For*.

Van Sant is quoted as saying, 'There was a mix-up between River Phoenix's agent and my producer, Laurie Parker, as to exactly what *My Own Private Idaho* was going to be, because there was another script, called *Revolver*, that somebody was offering River with my name attached. The agent [Iris] didn't know why the producer of *My Own Private Idaho* didn't know about *Revolver*. She assumed that *My Own Private Idaho* was some sort of trick and she wouldn't let us speak to River. But somehow we found him and I talked to him about the project.'

Snyder, however, was convinced about *Boogie Nights*, firmly believing it had Oscar potential written all over it. Sensing that Burton was calmer after reading the script, he was happy to receive a call from Joaquin asking for a meeting to be set up with the director. While liking the script, Joaquin still had concerns about the subject matter.

He would meet director Paul Thomas Anderson two days later at an Italian restaurant – and it seemed to have been a meeting that went well. Joaquin left the meeting interested but still with concerns, while the director was definitely interested in Joaquin.

Unfortunately, Iris just couldn't be convinced, and ultimately neither could Joaquin, who would eventually pass on the role. Snyder said, 'He had

Boogie Nights, that's what's so funny. The first person offered *Boogie Nights* was Leonardo DiCaprio, and he played around with it, wasn't sure about it but finally he passed. I liked the director so I had been pursuing it. After hearing that he passed I set up a meeting. He was still unsure about the role. And then the director sent over some documentary footage on the actor the movie was going to be based on, and he (Joaquin) started freaking out, saying, "I don't want to be in a porno, I can't be in a porno," and I was like, "It's not a porno. You have to understand, I get this movie."

'I was telling them, "You guys don't get it. This is a great director." I can see what he is going to do. But the point being, Joaquin got scared by the material and he didn't want to do it. Those things happen, but then he did the same thing with *American History X*,' revealed Snyder. 'We had one weekend – they were pulling the offer for (Ed) Norton and they offered it to us, but Joaquin was very afraid of the script. There was something about it, and I was like, "Come on guys, this is an Oscar role, I can smell it." And what happened was, Ed Norton and Mark Wahlberg then became his very strong competitors for other roles.'

While River would end up plumping for the sex comedy romp (although he would later regret it) of *A*

Night in the Life of Jimmy Reardon, the close-to-the-bone son-paying-for-his-father's-sins drama of *The Mosquito Coast* and a gay hustler in *My Own Private Idaho*, Joaquin seemed to have one eye on what people, or more importantly his family, thought about the roles he would take. Could it have been primarily because the acting focus was now on the younger Phoenix man, rather than the older one? Or maybe he was still latching onto the family blueprint and his mother's vision on what their calling was in Hollywood – and playing a porn star or Nazi skinhead wasn't quite on their wish-list of roles for him!

Explaining why he turned those sorts of projects down, Phoenix said, 'There's not many good scripts out there. I'll read a script and think, "Oh, this is terrible. They're never to get anyone to do it." Then I see who's doing it, and I'm shocked. Did I miss something? It's all very personal why you're attracted to do something.'

He added, 'I've often said that the role I got in *To Die For* was the best and worst thing for me. I wondered if I ever would escape from it. But I was confident that if I waited for the right films, it would work out.'

Undeterred, if Snyder couldn't get him those kind of risky and dangerous roles, the key was to find a film that had Joaquin as a romantic leading man, which is why they went for *Inventing The Abbotts* in 1997.

'The script was great,' explained Snyder. 'And I really liked the director Pat O'Connor, who had done an Irish film called *Circle of Friends*. It was just the film we need Joaquin to be going for.

'You're talking about an actor who has a great ability to morph into characters. He's not going to get normal studio roles. You have to play that studio thing to a degree. Because you can't get those smaller (independent) roles because you are not a name on the studio market. So we were very careful with Joaquin. Every film we got for Joaquin was very carefully planned out – who was directing it, who was in it, how it would be perceived.'

Inventing the Abbotts was important to Joaquin. In Iris's words, 'He needs a movie.'

CHAPTER FIVE

SO IT BEGINS

To Iris's relief, Joaquin would land the part of Doug who, according to Joaquin, was 'sixteen, kind of pudgy and just eats all the time so I put on weight for the role.'

Cast alongside him was Liv Tyler.

Liv said to the press shortly after *Inventing the Abbotts* was released, 'They couldn't find the guy for the part that Joaquin ended up playing. It was around the time I was finishing up on *That Thing You Do*, and I was getting worried. Then Pat (O'Connor, the director) called me one day and said, "I met this guy, and I think he's fantastic. I'd love for you to meet him. His name's Joaquin Phoenix." I was like, "Oh my God, why didn't I think of that? This is perfect." And I just fainted on my hands and knees. I walked into the room. He had his back to me. He looked at me and I just went, "Wheeeew." I had this grin on my face that was so silly. I couldn't get it to go away, one of those grins that actually hurts. I couldn't make a straight face. I had to leave the room. I just loved him. We talked all day.'

From the moment they met in rehearsals it was obvious to Joaquin that something was going to happen between them – whether close friends or something more. He was a single man again, and not particularly enjoying it. He would moan about potential girlfriends, 'I met a girl recently and we were out at dinner and suddenly she announces, "I'm vegan." I knew that was purely for my benefit because she got the information from a magazine and thought that was what she should say so we had something in common. You can see why meeting new people is so awkward. Normal things, like, "Are your parents together?" they already know. If I could make films and never do interviews or have my photo taken, I'd do it.'

However, he fell for Liv. Hard.

'We did hit it off immediately. I'm always surprised when there's a female person who thinks I'm attractive. With Liv, it was a totally natural thing. You see someone that you have great feelings for, and it's mutual – and that's that.'

He went to LA to work on the film, and soon the word was going around that there was huge chemistry between the two leads. The film's producer, Brian Grazer, had worked with a young Joaquin on *Parenthood*, and he recalled seeing the actor after all those years: 'He's got a fantastic and ridiculous sense of humour. I actually think he's a really good communicator. But I respond to emotional communication as opposed to highly articulate and eloquent communication. I find he uses body language a lot. I hadn't seen him for years, but he leaped over and hugged me. We're all a little damaged on the inside. He's a little damaged too. He just tries to protect that.'

Liv, who Joaquin would say in another interview that he was in complete 'awe' of during his experience on the film, added, 'I think he feels uncomfortable doing interviews and being around people he doesn't know. I understand, because you can't be completely honest. It's like thinking of the right thing to say, and not just acting on impulse.'

Liv's sister Mia said at the time, 'Liv's a little shy, and he just sweeps her off her feet and takes care of her. I could totally see them getting married.'

Liv said in interviews, 'We were so in love. We were

together every second, and we were the best of friends and in each other's trailers. Nobody knew – that's the amazing part.'

Despite it being a positive film set, he was still wrestling with his identity as an actor – striving to evolve as well as to figure out where he wanted his career to ultimately end. He would cast envious glances at his friend Leonardo DiCaprio, who was one of the planet's biggest stars thanks to the success of *Titanic*. But the jealously didn't stem from the adulation, but because DiCaprio had enough cache to do any project that he wanted. But, seeing it with first-hand experience from his brother, he was also aware that DiCaprio would have a hard journey trying to make a film where the audience could accept him being anything other than the one they fell in love with in James Cameron's blockbuster.

Retaining a sense of anonymity was essential to Phoenix. He could make the films that he wanted; he could evolve as an actor and take advantage of the flourishing indie scene at the time. 'It's tough. I just want to be right in the middle,' he said.

The indie scene of the 1990s kick started a whole new flurry of activity in the underground American cinema scene. While Joaquin wouldn't star in any of the classic films of that time, their success paved the way for other filmmakers to try out different kind of scripts – and it was exactly the sort of breakthrough he needed. While good looking, his appearance and demeanour was a blend of those silver screen heart-throbs – the mumbling, almost incomprehensible sounds of Marlon Brando and the stark impassioned pleas of James Dean.

As Vince Vaughn once noted, 'He goes to extreme emotional places. He can look like a scared, vulnerable child. Also like the guy in the pool room you don't want to mess with.'

Joaquin said once, 'I'm one of those actors who likes to stay in character between takes. I drive other actors crazy but, to me, the most important thing when I'm making a film is that the character takes precedence. I become obsessed with whoever I'm playing. I want to explore the character as completely as I can.'

But still those leading-man scripts would prove elusive. To make him more high profile, the idea was to get him to be the face of Prada. The fashion house had a reputation for casting against the grain – to go for anti-models, if you will. It was a perfect fit for Joaquin.

The shoot in Italy would be Joaquin and Liv's first proper public announcement that they were together. And Iris would later moan that Liv got all the perks, like amazing hotel rooms and free Prada gear instead of her.

Talking about his modelling career, Joaquin told *GQ* magazine, 'It was a career move. As an actor you want to show different sides, and I've very much gotten stuck being Jimmy in *To Die For*, because I wear second-hand clothing, or I did. And so the idea was, "Wow, it would be great to have photos out there with this slicked-down image and all that shit", and that's really why I did it. And they were very nice, and I think it probably accomplished what I wanted it to accomplish. But I didn't know what the fuck I was thinking, to tell you the truth.

'I think there's a certain amount of compromising that you must do to achieve what you want. I have more of a voice and more of an opportunity to express concerns about important subjects being in the position I am in than if I weren't. That's the balance you have to deal with. Now I can take money that I earn and donate it to groups that are doing amazing work, and do the commercials I did for PETA, which I wouldn't have the opportunity to do otherwise.'

He added that when he did the Prada campaign the stylist wore the shoes. 'They did a separate shot of the shoes and it wasn't me. You know, it's kind of ridiculous because who the hell's going to know that?' He bears no ill-will to Prada footwear, though. 'They make nice shoes. I tried to get them to make a vegetarian shoe, but no.'

He summarised his modelling career as, 'I did an advertising campaign for Prada but I haven't done a lot of modelling. I honestly didn't care that much about it. I went to Milan, some people put some stuff in my hair, I did this pose, we took some pictures and then they put it in the magazine with the Prada logo in, and that's it. I got some nice free clothes and I had a blast.'

While *Inventing the Abbotts* didn't set the box office alight ('The studio did a terrible marketing on it. They just threw it out there,' said Snyder. 'Studios have a hard time knowing what to with those kind of films.'), no one seemed to notice as all the focus was on Joaquin and Liv. It was a brand new experience for Joaquin. Suddenly, he was no longer the younger brother of River; he was one half of one of the coolest couples in Hollywood.

Everyone wanted a piece of Joaquin, and he and Liv would be ever-present figures in some of the trendiest LA clubs. She was more outgoing to the press than he was, and her career was certainly flying – thanks to the success of films like *Stealing Beauty*. On one occasion, after causing a storm at the Cannes film festival for the premiere of the film, she was greeted first by a driver, and then Joaquin standing there with a bunch of flowers in his hands.

Early word on *Inventing the Abbotts* was good, and Phoenix's Prada campaign was good too.

The shadow of River still lingered, though, and Joaquin would become irked at the constant questions asking if he drew on personal experiences to play Doug in the film – a young man who is trying to move out of his older brother's shadow.

He was then approached to star in Oliver Stone's quirky crime thriller *U Turn* (1997).

Talking about the script, upon reading it, he couldn't help just smiling to himself, saying, 'This is the shit.' The character was an odd man, among a whole town of odd men – in this case, a possessive boyfriend called Toby N. Tucker – which explained the TNT shaved into the back of his head. Snyder himself wasn't enthralled with the script but thought that it was a good part for Joaquin, and the chance to work with Stone would be a good one.

It was certainly different to see Joaquin have real fun with the character, as did most of the actors in the film – including a barely recognisable Billy Bob Thornton as a mechanic. Said Stone, 'His character is a real ass kicker, always feigning macho-hood but doesn't really have it. He totally pulls it off.'

Before setting off to do *U Turn* he was given a script for a film called *The Yards* (2000).

Phoenix loved it, and wanted a meeting set up with the director James Gray. After the meeting it was agreed Joaquin would play the main role of Leo Handler. Benicio del Toro was mentioned for the other role of Gutierrez. However, there was the small issue of financing, so Joaquin went on to work on *U Turn* in the hope that *The Yards* would eventually get made.

Working on *U Turn* saw him star alongside Sean Penn, an experience that he warmed to greatly – saying at the time, 'I'm nuts about him. I came onto the set about a month after they'd started shooting and I was terrified because they shot everything so quickly.

'Sean was an absolute veteran actor sweetheart – he took me under his wing, calmed me down and said nice things to me. He very much put me at ease. He's a wonderful, intelligent fellow who shared some of his poetry, about memory.'

He added about the film, 'It's a film noir. Sean Penn is this drifter who comes into this little town, and I'm one of the townies who makes him realise how much he needs to leave the town. My character is just a drama queen. Tight jeans, hair sticking up about two feet high, TNT shaved into the back of my head, black boots. This kid is nuts, a small-town bully living in a dream world. He's one of these people who feels the camera is on him all the time, that he's being watched and recorded.'

He would eventually label it as 'a weird gig' and with Stone's shooting style on this film favouring hand-held cameras, there would be no close-ups or long shots – the cameras were always on him and he felt exhausted, despite it being a short shoot.

A leading-man role in *Inventing the Abbotts* and a supporting performance in *U Turn* – not to mention the publicity surrounding his model shoot and his romance with Liv – was certainly reaping rewards.

Next up was *Clay Pigeons*, in 1998, alongside Vince Vaughn.

Clay Pigeons starts off with a bang. Literally, as Joaquin Phoenix's small-town character Clay shoots at bottles of Budweiser hanging from a tree. The opening scene is a delight – Phoenix's character is confronted by his friend Earl, accusing him of sleeping with his wife. The scene ends with a film noir dilemma – Earl killing himself but deliberately making it look like he was murdered by Clay.

David Dobkin's film is a delightful film noir tale

Clockwise, from top left: A ten-year-old Joaquin appeared alongside his sister Summer in an episode of *Murder She Wrote* in 1984; in 1986 in his film debut in *SpaceCamp*, directed by Harry Winer; looking just like his older brother River in 1989, the year he appeared in *Parenthood*; a 21-year-old Joaquin appeared alongside best friend Casey Affleck and Alison Folland in Gus Van Sant's black comedy, *To Die For* (1995).

Top left: Phoenix played Max California in Joel Schumacher's dark thriller, *8MM* (1999).

Top right: Phoenix gained much critical acclaim for his performances as Commodus in Ridley Scott's epic *Gladiator* (2000), gaining Oscar, Bafta and Golden Globe nominations.

Bottom: He played Merrill Hess alongside Mel Gibson in *Signs* (2002).

Top left: Phoenix appeared as Ray Elwood in the critically acclaimed *Buffalo Soldiers* (2001).

Top right and bottom: Phoenix co-starred alongside Adrien Brody in M. Night Shyamalan's *The Village* (2004) in which he played Lucius Hunt.

Top left: Joaquin holds aloft his Golden Globe award for Best Actor for his performance as Johnny Cash in *Walk the Line* (2005).

Top right: Joaquin at the 2006 Oscar ceremony alongside his mother and sister, Heart and Summer Phoenix.

Bottom: Phoenix's co-star Reese Witherspoon won the Best Actress Oscar for her portrayal of June Carter Cash in *Walk the Line*.

with a difference – clumsy dialogue rather than the hard-boiled variety, darkly comic instead of deadly serious, and bright unflinching daylight replacing the normally dark hues of this genre. It was filmed under Ridley Scott and his brother Tony's production company Scott Free.

Director Dobkin knew he had a great script in his hands, but because it was such a quirky subject he made sure that all emphasis was on the script, going over and over it until it was as perfect as it could be. 'Creatively, my inspiration was the Coen Brothers' *Fargo*, which took a classic, rather shallow situation and turned it into something new,' he said. 'I mean, nobody in *Fargo* has "a character arc", nobody really "learns anything", in Hollywood terms. But you always have the sense that these people have rich, full interior lives, a true philosophical depth, even if they live in a little town, even if they talk differently from you and I.'

Joaquin said about the proposed film, 'When I first read the script, I thought, "Wow, this could be really tough. In the wrong hands, it could just become preposterous." But then I met David, and we really hit it off. I immediately knew he had what it took to help us make these people come alive.'

Vaughn has described his character in an interview

thus: 'Lester is a guy who isn't necessarily from the west – that's just an image he's created of himself. Whatever his reality is, being badly hurt by women or whatever, he's made it over, taking bits and pieces of things he's seen in movies. He sees his life as a strange western movie, with himself as the hero. He thinks he's a sane person in an insane world. When I met David Dobkin I didn't know him, I read the screenplay and thought it was interesting. He convinced me in that first meeting to do the movie because he had such a specific idea on the story. He talked about the camera in a way that I didn't even understand back then. I just really took to him right away.'

He continued, 'I'm very fond of *Clay Pigeons*, yeah. I think he did a great job with that. And it was a fun character to play as well.'

In a People online interview, Dobkin said this about the characters: 'I wanted everyone to be different than what they appear to be – the FBI agent who smokes pot, the small-town sheriff who seems slow but is the one who figures (the murders) out in the end.'

Joaquin's small-town loser being sized up by Vaughn's out-of-town serial killer sees some great chemistry between the pair, and they would end up becoming close friends – much like Joaquin and Casey Affleck had become after *To Die For*.

'I think we genuinely like each other,' said Vaughn. 'Acting means a lot to him, and I respect that, because it means a lot to me.' There was something else that seemed to be right too. 'We were, like, reduced to twelve-year-olds when we'd hang out with each other. When we were filming it was like summer camp.'

Phoenix again impressed. He was rooted into the character, despite the madness that floats around him. It also helped that he and Vaughn had huge chemistry. He would say about working with Vaughn, 'Well, it was a great cast. I think Vince is a blast – very charming, very funny. He was such a sweetie. Um, so we really have this little family. You always kind of have these families when you're working, but this was a low-budget film shooting in a really small town in Utah, and we're all staying at the same motel, so me, and Janeane [Garofalo], we're neighbours, and we're just kind of leaving the door open, and everybody walks around. So, there's really a tight group and David Dobkin directed it, [he's] just one of the sweetest guys.'

Phoenix added, 'The amount of time – we shot *Clay Pigeons* in six weeks with six-day weeks – was really brutal. It was a much longer shoot for *8MM* [a later film]. Here's the thing: In *8MM* you get the trailer; it's grand. In *Clay Pigeons*, they say, "If you don't mind, share with Vince, because your trailer's been repossessed. Literally."'

During the film Dobkin noted that in a fishing scene Joaquin refused to put the fish on the hook. And when the film's director enquired whether Joaquin would be interested in a film he was thinking about, which would require Joaquin to play a bullfighter, he responded, 'Absolutely not. The only way I'll do if is if the bull wins and kills me in the end.'

Finally, it looked like Joaquin would sign up for *The Yards* after all.

Talking about *The Yards*' director James Gray, Phoenix said, 'I'm not sure if I'd seen *Little Odessa* before I met him, or if I was told to see it around that time. Actually, I first heard about *The Yards* because of Liv. She had all her scripts from CAA at the apartment, and one day I lifted the cover off of one of about a thousand scripts that she had and it said *The Yards*.

'And I turned to her and said, "The titles of your scripts are better than any I've been getting." There was something mysterious and ambiguous about the title, *The Yards*. And that was it. Then a couple of weeks later, my agent called and said, "I have a script called *The Yards*." I said, "Yeah, I know that title." I read the script then and thought it was amazing. When

James came to New York to meet me I just felt he was somebody whom I could genuinely trust, which needless to say is very important for an actor. And I also just liked my character's trajectory.'

Phoenix's decision not to make *Boogie Nights* would haunt him. Wahlberg, fresh from the success of that film, was going to play Gutierrez in *The Yards*. However, alarm bells began to ring when Phoenix received a phone call from Gray asking if he spoke Spanish. Immediately, suspicions were raised as there was no Spanish in the script. Not long after, Gray asked Phoenix what he thought about playing the role of Gutierrez instead of Leo. It was clear that the role earmarked for him was going to Mark Wahlberg instead. It seemed it was a power play by Wahlberg's agents. He was the bigger star, and the bigger star should get the bigger role.

Snyder added, 'I think that with everything, the more successful you get... The whole thing was just an agency power play to show Mark Wahlberg how powerful they could be, like, "We can get that for you."

Speaking to Contactmusic.com about the casting, and that each of the three principles had their own stigmas – Wahlberg with his Marky Mark days, Phoenix and his brother stigma, and Theron struggling to escape her beauty – Gray said, 'See, the style of movies have changed so much since the period when I enjoyed them. OK, say the year is 1973 and I want to make this movie. A) It's easier for me to raise the money. B) If I want to cast it, I can look on the stage, I can go to Lee Strasberg and say "What actors you got for me?" If I'm trying to make that kind of social realist movie today, how do I cast this movie? I cannot go by actor's "reputations". What I can go by is whether the actor has shown in other movies a level of total commitment, and also a certain emotional awareness – a depth, a sensitivity. If I can perceive that, I don't care what their reputation is. I'm going to cast them.'

Gray also said, 'The truth of the matter is that it's very difficult to make this kind of movie. The evidence is all around you. Somewhere around 1980, there was a horrible perversion of the art form where somebody said, "If you can summarise a movie in four words you've got a great movie." This is one of the worst ideas in the history of the planet.

'I spend a lot of my time trying to resist categorisation. I love film noir in cinema. Abraham Polonsky's *Force of Evil* is one of my favourite movies. But that seems to be the domain of the detective movie. What I was anxious to do was more of a social drama, which seems a genre that died. Something like *On the Waterfront*.'

Gray explained that he'd discussed with Wahlberg

the big chance he took with *The Yards*. 'He's an anti-hero in the mythical sense. It's a very risky thing to do because it's totally underplayed. It's not the kind of guy who is the star and gets the girl. It's a much more risky thing. With Joaquin, he's a totally committed actor and he doesn't mind going down into the darkest place. Charlize, too. I mean, Charlize is a very trained actor. I was blown away by her, consistently. So I feel like they are often hostage to movies that don't take advantage of what they can do.'

It's clear the gritty crime thriller meant a lot to Joaquin – the backlash to the desperate need for the youth of America to define success based on ownership of materialistic things would have appealed to Joaquin and his family. To Joaquin the New York shoot was an appealing one too, with the added bonus he had a director who knew how to push his buttons. They would shoot in New York subways, heading down into the deep catacombs, with the summer heat searing through their bones, only to find Gray constantly uttering, 'One hundred per cent emotional commitment', to keep the intensity rising as much as the heat.

Joaquin would respond to the constant mantra, just as he did for the preparation before and after the shoot. It's an actorly cliché, usually aided by the rolling of the eyes at whoever utters it, but he would immerse himself in the character – to the point where not only would he find it hard to shake him off, but he would lose contact with friends for a while because of his odd behaviour.

'It's about the falsity of the American dream. It's an odd thing that my generation faces; we're encouraged to pursue the American dream but we don't really have the right moral support to make those decisions. So you have this character Willie. We know nothing of his parents bar one reference early on to his mother. You really get a sense that there's this child who has had to grow up really quick and hard. It's about betrayal and friendship and love, and how those outside forces can pollute our relationships,' he explained.

'Any actor who says that he or she had to leave that character at home on the weekend is full of shit and pretentious. It's more subtle than that. That's when you see through a performance, when it's all show. There's not one process for either getting into a role or out of it that I have found. For *The Yards*, it wasn't until a year afterwards that I looked back and wondered how I did it.'

For *The Yards* he hired a trainer, to work him for six days a week – in order to, as Joaquin would put it, 'feel every muscle in his body'.

'On the treadmill I thought my shins were going to explode. It's the best... he added.

He wanted to look like a Calvin Klein model – ironic, given Wahlberg's involvement.

There was a scene in the movie requiring Phoenix to perform something dramatic. He would head to the other side of the set and smash his head onto a piece of oak on the wall, causing a huge welt to appear. Gray was told by a nurse on the set that Phoenix was banging his head on the wall. He understandably rushed to where he was, to indeed find his actor thrashing his head against the wall. The incident is a well-worn tale in Hollywood, and while he has resorted to that sort of intense preparation on more than one occasion, he is rankled by how the press portray him:

'The press has just gone out of their way to insist that every day, in addition to brushing my teeth and taking a shower, I bang my head against the wall in preparation. Which I just find odd because one day on the *The Yards* and another on *Return to Paradise*, I had some tense, emotional scenes, and you're standing around with people drinking coffee and saying, "Did you see the game last night?" So you're thinking, "How the fuck do I get into this (heavy) place right?" So I do something extreme, but suddenly that defines me, and it's totally inaccurate, because that's one moment. And they cut out the rest.'

Gray told *GQ*, 'Joaquin is willing to put himself into

the most troubling and personal and exposing of places, which is all you can ask from an actor. Frankly, it's very difficult for me to work with him – I'm not comfortable with torture.'

He later added, 'But I will work with him in a second, because he's that good.'

Said Joaquin of Gray, 'It's the sense that you are going to go in and try to discover things in a different way than you might with other directors. It's what he's interested in, what he values and he pushes you hard because he pushes himself in the same way. I cannot say how easy it is for a director to go "cut, print" and walk off.'

He would typically go all out to make a fight scene with Wahlberg convincing. He said, 'Mark and I blocked it out of ourselves. We wanted it to be an epic battle, falling down the stairs and out on to the street. We had elbow pads and knee pads, but on the first take Mark just grabbed me with his pinkie, flipped me into the air and I landed on my head. Man, did I have a bump. I was black and blue for days. But I sure as hell wasn't gonna do any fucking John Wayne-style punching. I wanted it to be sloppy and barbaric and painful, like I'm hugging the life out of this guy who's my friend while I'm pounding at him.'

Talking about Wahlberg, Joaquin added, 'He's a genius. I know this sounds dramatic, but when you go through months of working together under odd circumstances, you build a bond that's like during war. Well, maybe not war, but basic military training. When I'm done with a movie, I want to walk away and not have anything to do with it for a while. So it's always an odd thing, the friendships you make.'

In an interview with internet newspaper *The Huffington Post* Gray spoke about how he came to cast Joaquin: 'I first met Joaquin in 1997, on a cold winter night in New York. It was a blustery and brutal evening after a brutal day, and I'd had nothing less than a brutal week trying to cast my film *The Yards*. I'd met with what seemed like a hundred actors, and most of them seemed talented and enthusiastic. But what they all lacked – for me, anyway – was a certain quality that separates the best from the rest: an ability to communicate a complex inner life.'

However, he knew after only a few moments of conversation, that Joaquin was that person. 'He was conflicted, he was bright, and he was hungry. Something else was obvious, too: Joaquin had danger. I wasn't scared of him, but I was scared of what he might do, most of all to himself. I had to work with him as soon as possible.

'Looking back on our first collaboration, I'm not sure we actually collaborated all that much. I seem to remember a whole lot of torment and angst and yelling and screaming. But I also remember consistently being amazed by the emotional depth of the then twenty-four-year-old, and I loved his feral unpredictability. He seemed ready to explode at any minute.'

Joaquin, he said, was hard on himself, a true perfectionist. 'We had one thing in common, and that was a total commitment to the work. We will no doubt fail, we told each other over and over again, but at least we will fail giving it everything we have. He was untrained and undisciplined, usually requiring multiple takes and a great deal of coaching. So did I. *The Yards* feels now like the first round of a boxing match in which neither fighter seems ready to engage.'

Gray would liken working together with Joaquin to being a devil perched on his shoulder – coaxing and jibing him to get a reaction, finger jabbing him until he would give Gray a look to suggest that he was ready for the cameras to role.

However, Gray took it too far on one occasion where he would use his relationship with Tyler to act as some sort of motivation for an intense scene – asking him how he would react if she died in his arms. It was too much for Phoenix, who berated the director for taking it too far, saying, 'Aw James, you had me in the zone, and you ruined it. You ruined it.'

Director Joel Schumacher would later say about working with Phoenix, 'Joaquin understands the danger of this business. I've worked with several young actors I have worried about, and I'm not worried about him at all. I knew River, who was also talented, just very different, and I've often wondered if having an older brother gave Joaquin perspective – it's just a guess.'

Schumacher's observation wasn't without merit. He did, after all, create the early Brat Pack film *St Elmo's Fire*, as well as being the one responsible for pairing Corey Feldman and Corey Haim on screen in *The Lost Boys*.

Commenting on his brother's constant change of appearance, sister Rain said, 'It's an understatement to say he gets into a part, because Joaquin always goes full throttle. It's wild to see how he changes. One day he looks really college, two weeks later he has blue hair.'

He seemed adept at playing strange or simple characters and he impressed with his charisma in *The Yards*, but in *Return to Paradise*, he would play a relatively everyday man jailed for drug possession in Malaysia.

Phoenix explained how it came about: 'I asked what Joseph Ruben was doing next and he said this film, which was essentially amazing. And I said I'd love to read the script, but nothing ever came of it. I'm not sure why, and then a few months later my agent sent me this script. I read it and found out that this was something Vince [Vaughn] was doing. Ruben didn't know that we had worked together. He didn't know we were friends at all. And I said, "I just finished a film with him." And he said, "Oh, really? Do you like each other?" I said, "Yeah, he's a good guy." So, Vince called me a couple of days later and said, "I can't believe this, you're doing this movie." He didn't really know what was happening.'

Ruben added, 'I called Vince up and he asked who you getting to play my friends, and I said, "A guy called Joaquin Phoenix," and he said, "You're joking? You know I'm really good friends with him. You're kidding me? That's so fucking fantastic."

'I had no idea they were so close. And it was great because they liked each other so much, which helps when they are playing friends.'

Return to Paradise would be a 'What would you do?' kind of drama, which begins with the story of three characters, played by Vince Vaughn, Phoenix and David Conrad, enjoying a backpacking trip in Malaysia. The beachfront house is the temporary base where they while away their time together drinking, taking drugs and generally enjoying themselves. However, when they part ways, two of them return to America, while Phoenix's character Lewis McBride, decides to head to Borneo for some environmental activism.

However, Vaughn's Limo driver character, Sheriff, is stunned to find out that when they left, their beach home was raided and Lewis has been imprisoned for two years. He and Conrad's character are faced with a dilemma – they must serve time in prison for three years each to share the burden or Lewis will be executed. You can understand why Phoenix would take the part. He only appears sporadically, but his scenes have huge impact.

As always, he would take the role incredibly seriously, appearing on-set gaunt and looking like he was wasting away. A stunned Joseph Ruben took him aside, not to see if he was all right, but because he was hoping to shed a few pounds himself and wanted to ask him for diet tips – to which Phoenix would reply dryly, 'It's easy. Just stop eating.'

It would be easy to dismiss his performance as the one with the most opportunity to stand out in the movie, but in reality, Vaughn, Anne Heche and Jada Pinkett Smith all have chances to shine in a script that, while treading a formulaic line, does offer an opportunity for the leads to play less-than-perfect characters.

But it's Joaquin who seizes it fully, culminating in a couple of truly heartfelt moments, particularly his plea to camera. Through a mixture of script and instinct he wisely refused to play the character as philosophical but as a real man caught in a horrific situation. He wants to live, and he has no dignity left to even pretend otherwise.

The scene, and his performance in general, would be somewhat tarnished by the insinuation that he was almost exploiting his brother's death to get to the emotional depths needed for the film. It is, of course, an accusation that would hurt – but Joaquin is keen to point out that he wouldn't be able to cope with going to that particular well every time he needed to fuel an intense scene, and that he had proved he could do emotional scenes in other films before his brother's death.

Schumacher would say about his performance, 'The reason that *Return to Paradise* works on some level is because you care about getting this boy out.'

Revealing how he came to cast Joaquin, director Ruben revealed, 'Joaquin at the time was an upcoming actor. Normally at that level as an actor he would come in and read. But his agent said he won't do readings, but can we do it as a meeting instead. I agreed.

'But he was so shy, he barely talked. We just kind of sat there and smiled at each other. He was so innately sympathetic. Your heart just went out to him. That was exactly what the role needed. And we barely spoke but he got the role.'

He added, 'I had seen *Inventing the Abbotts* and liked it. It's always nice to see them read in character but I had total confidence in him.'

As in *The Yards,* Joaquin went to some dark places for the film.

Ruben said, 'Well, Joaquin puts himself into a role so completely. In one scene he is being dragged by guards to his death, to be hung. It was incredibly emotional, and Joaquin literally starting banging his head against the walls to get into this nightmarish place that he needed to go.'

He went on to describe the making of the scene: 'We shot all his coverage and it was all so horrifically emotional. We then had to film Vince's reaction shots. It usually means the other actor would play out the role behind the camera. But Joaquin was putting himself through the same preparation off camera, the same horrific and screaming performance. It was just as good as what he did on camera.

'Vince came up to me and said, "He doesn't need to put himself through this."

'I said to Joaq, "You don't have go through this. You don't have to go all the way back into that place. Vince is fine."

'And he turned to me, and said, "If I don't go all the way, I feel like an asshole."

'I knew exactly what he meant. As a person, he's shy and a little self-conscious. When he acts he has to completely be there, completely in character, or he'll get self-conscious.

'He was so extreme. At one point he discussed getting a couple of tough guys putting him in a room for a couple of days and roughing him up in the middle of the night to simulate what his character went through in Malaysia. But I was like, "We don't need to do that. I ain't going to put you through that."'

Ruben also gave an example of Joaquin's crazy, funny side: 'We were shooting in Hong Kong at this fancy hotel. And we're leaving down this elegant carpeted stairway. He falls, rolls down the stairway. It's crazy but funny. It was great. He likes to play, he's playful.'

Joaquin did wryly admit, however, that 'The crew probably thought I was a little mad.'

Critically, Phoenix received more praise than the actual film.

Critic Roger Ebert noted, 'Vince Vaughn as Sheriff, is now working as a limo driver. He doesn't have much of a life, but at least it's his. Tony is engaged to be married. As for Beth, we only gradually learn her full story, which catches Sheriff in a tricky emotional vice; Joaquin Phoenix as the prisoner, is not stoic or philosophical, but feels the way most people would when a death sentence appears out of the blue.'

While CNN said, 'Phoenix is truly great, looking like he's been run through a wringer every day for two years, babbling endlessly about the absence of God in his prison cell. (This guy is dating Liv Tyler, so he's obviously acting.)

Phoenix was getting steady work, and they were all interesting projects. And he would be working again very soon.

He recounted the tale: 'I hadn't seen my agent for a long time, so I went over to her place and we were talking about *Return to Paradise*, the fact that it was happening, and trying to figure out what to do following that, what would be the best move. She said, "I'd like you to do something bigger with a studio." I said, "You know, I just want to do a good film, whatever may come along." And we're sitting talking and the phone rings and it's Joel Schumacher, who she knows. And she says, "I'm sitting here with Joaquin Phoenix." And he goes, "Well great, that's why I'm calling. I have this script and I want him to read it and talk a little bit about it," and he wanted to meet me. So I went over and met him.'

Talking about his character in *8MM* (1998), the project Schumacher wanted to see him about, Phoenix said, 'Nic Cage is a private detective hired when someone finds a snuff film in her husband's safe; she wants to know if it's real and if so who's the girl and who are the men who killed her. So he comes to Los Angeles, where I work in a sex shop, and I become his guide to all these underground places. My character is really sad – a character in a tragic situation is sad, but one who doesn't know it is worse.'

He continued, 'We get in way over our heads. I think it's great that he's paying me money, and I'm happy for that and to be out of the sex shop; I really think I'm a big man. But I'm ridiculous – I have vinyl pants and pierced eyebrows and blue hair. He's such a sad little punk, he wants to be a rocker, to be Jim Morrison but he's got zero talent, he's never going to make it, so he has to laugh about it, to make jokes. He thinks that they're like a great team – Starsky and Hutch or Jon and Poncherello.'

Joaquin was finally earning money for himself, and not having to rely on anyone else.

'It's a great job and you work and it's great. But I do put a lot of work into what I do and it consumes my thoughts for months, and recovering from that is even more terrible,' he said.

'I think that you are allowed to spend the ridiculous amounts of money that you make on bullshit things that don't really matter just because you want to as long as you balance that with giving back, which I think that I do. I think about my friend who's evicted because he can't pay his rent in his apartment and I just tossed out $500 for a MiniDisc player because I wanted a MiniDisc player so I could record my own music. It's bizarre. I don't know, it's all relative. I don't have the answers. I'm just still trying to figure it out.

'Well, in comparison to my friend who got evicted, yes, I'm filthy stinking rich, and he thinks "If I only had that I'd be set for life." Well, I look at whatever actor and go, "You son of a bitch, if I got paid that for every fucking movie I ever made, are you kidding? I'd buy a whole city block and set up housing for, you know, whatever." So, it's all relative and I don't, I don't make that much money.'

Talking about what he was doing with his money, he said, 'Right now, really, I'm establishing a comfortable home for myself and my family and for my nephew and for whatever groups I can donate to help them out, to keep them alive. I'll do that as much as it is realistic. I think that you try the best that you can, but we're all selfish, we all want something fabulous for ourselves and want to make it. I know people that are like, "I would never do one of those Japanese commercials for a million dollars, two million dollars." Screw you. Goddamn right I'll do a commercial for two million dollars.'

It wasn't all great news, however. Early word wasn't good on *The Yards*, and it was around this time that he and Liv broke up.

When they finally split up after nearly three years together, Joaquin said rather eloquently, 'And I know that when Liv and I met it was for a reason – I really needed her and she really needed me. And at a certain point, I think we stopped evolving with each other, stopped progressing, and made a very mature decision to move on, even though there was still a great love there.'

He told *GQ*, 'People move in and out of your life when both need it. When I met her, she certainly had this spunk, this kind of zest for life and excitement about the future. And at that point, I suppose, I was bitter about a lot of things: about my brother and the press and how ugly everything seemed. Liv helped change my perspective, and that was a great thing.'

Re-shoots were needed on *The Yards*. And it looked like they would be extensive.

At this time Snyder noticed a change in Phoenix. He was expecting roles to come to him, and with other agencies circling there were concerns that he would leave the Burton agency. He wanted the scripts that were going to A-list stars – the ones that had made their mark on the box office. He was still searching for that elusive project.

CHAPTER SIX

THUMBS UP FOR JOAQUIN

S nyder heard word on a film called *Gladiator* (2000). Initially the word was that Ed Norton was being lined up for the role of the Roman Emperor Commodus, so Snyder thought there was little chance of Phoenix even getting a meeting, never mind the actual part, and put it aside.

However, after hearing they were still looking for an actor, he contacted DreamWorks for the script. It was a script that had several writers (and would go on to have more) and featured a genre that Hollywood had forgotten about: *Gladiator* had a star director.

His films may not have always set the box office alight, but Ridley Scott's vision heralded the haunted-house-in-space scare-fest that was *Alien* and the hugely influential sci-fi classic that is *Blade Runner*. His failures were by and large flawed efforts rather than run-of-the-mill ones – and he was one of the few directors capable of bringing the Roman Colosseum to epic, sweeping life.

The villain of the piece was remarkably complex for a Hollywood blockbuster. Commodus was a spoiled, petulant brat grasping for power.

Crowe would say about the environment, 'On the set of *Gladiator*, I didn't have a very good relationship with the producer. I had a very good relationship with Ridley, but the producers couldn't understand why I wouldn't just chill out. The reason I wouldn't chill out was because I knew if I did fucking chill out, in those five minutes something stupid would now be in the movie. Like, they were trying to get me to do a love scene, and I'm saying to them, "What we're doing here is about the vengeance of a man whose wife has been killed, you cannot have him stop off for a little bit of nookie on the way."'

The film came about through screenwriter David Franzoni. He had been given a three-picture deal with DreamWorks studio based on the success of his screenplay for Steven Spielberg's *Amistad* with them. He mentioned the idea of *Gladiator* to Steven Spielberg, who asked three questions, Franzoni recalled: 'It was about ancient Roman gladiators, not American, Japanese, whatever else? Yes, I said. Taking place in the ancient Coliseum? Yes. Fighting with the swords and animals to the death and such? Yes. Great, let's make this movie.'

Franzoni had the idea for the film after reading the 1958 novel *Those About to Die* by Daniel Mannix. His screenplay had the protagonist Narcissus (as he was named then) become something of a superstar gladiator who is sponsored by the Golden Pompeii Olive Oil Company. An advertising slogan has the line: 'Narcissus would kill for a taste of Golden Pompeii Olive Oil'.

'My vision from the beginning was this is not *Ben-Hur*. It's *All Quiet on the Western Front*. This is a grown up movie about war, death and life in Rome – the life of a gladiator. I would have liked to have had more fun with this,' he would say, referring to the elimination of the Olive Oil company endorsement.

Franzoni explained, 'In 1995, I was in Rome, writing *Amistad*, brainstorming *Gladiator*, when I read the 'Augustan Histories'. In it, it describes how Emperor Commodus would actually partake in gladiator contests himself in the Coliseum. And that a slave named Narcissus had been the one who had killed

Commodus. Well, this was my story, my way in: who was this Narcissus? There was nothing historically written about the guy, but I knew he was going to be the hero of the story I was going to write. I would invent his life.'

A second draft by John Logan turned it into a more serious affair, while William Nicholson became the film's third writer. *Gladiator: Film and History* author Martin Winkler said, 'It seems rather likely that it was Scott who turned the film from Franzoni's socio-political, delightfully bizarre action film into a more sombre study of war, death and life in Rome.'

The screenplay would go through many more changes, even when the cameras were rolling. 'Last minute tweaking of the script and a new ending helped the production stay on track,' said producer Douglas Wick.

Scott was convinced he could resurrect the genre from the dead, saying after the film was released, 'There were a lot of epic films made in the 1940s and 1950s in Hollywood. After that people just stopped going to them and there was this fear of making period films for the big audience. That was one of the big challenges, actually. You couldn't make this film cheaply, but you could make it mainstream.

'Everybody was quietly sniggering that Roman epics of this nature went out forty-five years ago and that it wouldn't work. But I was absolutely confident about what I was going to do. Actually, I hadn't been that confident since *Alien*. It's funny, but when you are charging down to the fence and you know you are going to jump, there is a different level of exhilaration. And, yes, we had shortfalls – we were constantly behind on the writing – but we were never behind on the production.'

Soon Snyder had the script in his hands, and he was blown away by what he read.

Phoenix received a phone call from Snyder, urging him to get to the office as soon as possible. He had in his hands a script featuring a role that Joaquin if he could get it, no matter how unlikely, had Oscar chances.

As Burton's paranoia began to bubble over with her fear that other agencies were hovering over her young adult clients – like Phoenix, Kirsten Dunst and Josh Hartnett – just waiting to pounce, she was desperately showing frugalness. Scripts sent to her clients' houses via couriers were frowned upon, with Burton advising them to come to her office. She would also ask her clients to bring their own paper to cut back on the costs of faxing scripts – something that horrified Snyder, who would rather pay for paper at his own expense.

So Joaquin was forced to travel to the office on his motorbike – only to find Snyder waiting with a giddy smile and a promise that he had a role that would guarantee him an Oscar. 'Joaquin, just read these five pages. Just these five pages,' he said.

'And he read them – and I just said very slowly. This is an Oscar. Do it right and you've got it.'

His chances of getting the role were heightened significantly because Ridley liked Phoenix. He was impressed with him during the shooting of *Clay Pigeons*, which he executive-produced – and he wanted a meeting with the actor. In fact, he was more than impressed with him, and after watching him work in *Clay Pigeons* and then put in a powerhouse performance in *Return to Paradise* he was convinced that he was the right person for the part.

Ridley had already got his way casting Crowe, who had a no-nonsense, brash attitude – the exact opposite of Phoenix – but he was just as much a handful. Both took up a director's time – in Crowe's case by constantly questioning the script and the shot, while Phoenix would require careful handling.

In a Turkish newspaper, Joaquin said, 'Ridley told me, when I was doing *Clay Pigeons*, that I have an interesting and expressive face which suggests hatred, evil and treason, and that he could never think of anyone else than me for the role of Commodus. I replied, "Are you crazy? How could I possibly master that part?" Ridley suggested then that we should at least try to do a few scenes first. Then I asked Ridley why he wanted me for the part and he replied that he couldn't think of a more neurotic, paranoid young emperor. So we shook hands.'

In truth, it was never that easy.

A screen test was ordered, as although Scott was sure he had his man, he was meeting with reluctance from the studio. The subsequent screen test didn't get the reaction that he wanted. The studio still didn't see Joaquin in the role, and were suddenly keen on Jude Law, who was getting loads of positive feedback for his work on *The Talented Mr Ripley*. The only thing in Joaquin's favour was that Law's agents, according to Snyder, were asking for an offer and wouldn't screen-test.

Ridley managed to convince the studio to do another screen test with Joaquin in full gladiatorial regalia. But again, this test failed to get Joaquin the part.

It seemed now that the movie was on shaky ground, because star power wasn't available for the movie. Luckily, Universal stepped in to partner DreamWorks on the project.

Russell remarked in an *Empire* magazine interview in 2009, 'There wasn't a single person in Los Angeles who thought "Oh great!" I mean, everybody was kind of looking at me as though I was retarded, patting me on the back and saying, "Well you know, *L.A. Confidential* was great wasn't it? At least you got to be in one good one." And they were doing that all over town. I was like, "It's Ridley Scott! Are you aware of what he's capable of doing when it comes to creating a world."'

Before it was released, *Variety* stated, 'Even if the film is a big hit, it's unlikely that the genre will come back in any significant way due to the high costs involved.'

Snyder would say it was one of the longest waits he'd ever seen for one of his clients. After a few screen tests, Iris was getting tetchy, ordering Snyder to 'get the numbers of every producer, writer and the janitor at DreamWorks and Universal, and we are going to call every one of them until we find out who is holding up the deal.'

Within days Joaquin had the part.

DreamWorks' Steven Spielberg no doubt played his part – since he had used Burton's kids on several films including *ET* and *Hook*, as well as using River in *Indiana Jones and the Last Crusade*.

His first day proved to be an eye opener. On paper, it was an easy shot – simply walking towards the palace. He presumed it would be an easy day – a couple of wide shots. However, what he saw blew his mind away. 'I'd get there and see 150 troops, 200ft statues, three cameras, a crane, some camels. Which is when I thought: "Oh, so that's how you make an epic."'

He stressed the importance of Ridley's control: 'He is so patient and so calm. I don't know how he did it. He'd have five cameras running, five monitors, hundreds of extras. And he'd be watching all this. And I know that one of the cameras is just floating between me in the roll box [in the arena] *and* Lucilla, played by Connie Nielsen... And suddenly the radio would crackle, "Ridley's coming on." And he'd come up and say, "I like that thing that you did, try that again." And I was like, how the hell did you see that? You've got tigers attacking Russell over here, and somehow he's able to just balance all of it, take it all in, and edit in his mind.

'And even between takes, they'd be setting everything back up, and he'd be drawing the storyboards for the following day's work, or for the scenes that we were going to do. And they're works of art of themselves. They're beautiful – the detail.'

He loved working with Ridley, as he was someone who would talk to him between shots, asking him his opinion – even with all the madness of making an epic film. As he said, initially when he arrived on set Joaquin wondered what on earth he'd got himself into, but Ridley's calmness was felt by all involved. 'You just pick up on that energy,' Joaquin said. 'I mean, you certainly can feel if somebody seems overwhelmed and frenzied; and it's the last thing you want from a director when they're going into a five-month shoot with a picture like this.'.

Russell said of Phoenix, 'Joaquin is a lovely guy, but nervous. He lacks a little self-confidence. Ridley would say, "You're now the emperor and you have to walk out in the middle of the Colosseum." And Joaquin would say, "But I'm a lad from Florida. What do you want me to do? Wave?"'

Luckily, the late Richard Harris, who played his father in the film, would come up with a plan. 'Harris,' Russell recalled, 'with all his years and knowledge of the cinema and his wisdom, said quite simply, "Let's get him drunk!" And the drinking session seemed to do the trick. Joaquin kind of realised, "Oh yeah, I'm an actor, so I can relax a little bit."'

Phoenix said, 'Initially, I was not sure where to start. Going through the first rehearsal dressed in my jeans, I was thinking, "What the hell am I doing?" Then I put on the layers of armour and I felt different. Costume and make-up really do make a big difference, especially because I'm obsessed with the physicality of the character.

'At the beginning I permed my hair twice, to look

like the young scraggy prince in waiting. Then, as he became emperor I cut my hair and stopped going to the gym.'

He wanted to be muscular for the role, to pack on weight to play an emperor. But then realised that a man becoming greedy with power would become more decadent, so he stopped working out and tucked into huge dishes of pasta instead, and drunk the bottle of vodka near his bed before he went to sleep. A story went round claiming that Ridley looked at him through the monitor and uttered, 'Fuck he's fat.'

Phoenix recalled, 'I thought I wanted to be muscular for the film so I worked out for a couple months and put on more weight for the fight scenes. Then once I became Emperor we shot in sequence and I thought, "fuck all that, I'm not going to the gym!" I wanted to try out this decadent nature of his and I thought it might help me age a little bit. I really wanted him to be the young prince in waiting and then become more dishevelled as he becomes Emperor and alter his physical appearance, because you leave that story for a few months and it becomes Russell's journey. So I put on some weight there.'

Joaquin liked being secluded from the rest of the world in Malta where they were filming. It meant the cast could bond, rather than head off into their personal lives after the shoot had wrapped. For someone who has been brought up in the environment he has been, a sense of community was something he cherished, and it would also allow him to latch onto the cast and crew and create stability in an environment he was unsure of and insecure about.

Connie's place he treated like his personal historical library, as she had filled her place up with tons of historical books, while with Harris it would be sitting and listening intently to his stories.

He said, 'I had a very specific interpretation of the way I wanted to play it, but at first I didn't know if that would fit in with the rest of the characters in the film as a whole. Commodus is certainly a man-child, and he was a neglected child. It was very important for me to illustrate that in certain ways. His reactions to the combats in the arena – it's almost as if he doesn't comprehend what human life is; people are merely toys for his enjoyment.'

The film would see him tangle with Russell Crowe's hero character.

Crowe's fiery temperament is well known, but Joaquin warmed to the brusque New Zealander instantly. 'He's intense in the best way,' said Joaquin. 'He will stop at nothing to get a scene right, but off the set he was very generous with his time, always throwing parties for the cast and crew, renting sailboats and taking everybody out. Which was great, 'cause we were in Malta for three months on this film, with nothing else to do when we weren't working.

'It was the opposite of the relationship in the script Actually Russell isn't very talkative. He memorises his part incredibly well and is very meticulous. Even if Ridley was pleased with a particular scene, if Russell wasn't sure about it, he'd do the same scene again and again until he had found the perfection he was looking for. Apart from that, he's a great person. He's very confident and imperturbable.'

Talking about the character he added, 'Lucius Aurelius knows that he is evil. He kills his father and becomes emperor at the age of nineteen. Yet he is a psychopath. He is in love with his sister. He enjoys murdering people. In short, he is a very immoral boy. He comes to enjoy power at a very young age. His character is very unsteady; it changes constantly. For example, he wants the people to love him, but the gladiator fights which he organises to reach this end turn out to be fatal for himself in that they cause Maximus, whom he believes dead, to come to Rome and seal his fate.'

For the scene with his screen sister, Joaquin noted, 'I'm desperate. Me and Lucilla lie next to each other.

Then I lose control and get on top of her and at that moment Connie Nielsen, who plays the part of Lucilla, shouts at the camera, "I can't do that, I can't concentrate. I cannot forget that it is my brother that I'm supposed to be with. I can't do something that's so abnormal!" All of us, especially Ridley Scott, cannot get rid of the feeling that we have committed a sin while doing that scene.'

SpaceCamp director Harry Winer opined, 'The goal in acting is to be, rather than to act, and in being you reveal a certain part of yourself, and if you've got a part of yourself that is intriguing and draws people in, whether you're an evil son of a bitch or you've got a great sense of humour, or it's an openness that people find infectious – each star has a different one – that's what people latch onto. The audience then go to that well continuously in order to get a hit of that quality. When actors go into a casting room, you'll know immediately as soon as they open their mouths whether they have something.

'Joaquin has an openness that makes him charming. It's a commentary on life that adds layers and layers to this openness, which makes you unable to be as open but gives you new qualities – makes him compelling. When I think of him in *Gladiator*, which I think is one of the most brilliant performances I have ever seen by a young actor, I'll put it up against any performance I've ever seen. Even though his portrayal is complicated, jealous and vain, he is so compelling because there is a vulnerability. And because of that you cared about him. It was that vulnerability that made Leaf compelling from the get go. He has had that motif from the start and it's the bedrock of all the characters he plays. That's what makes him interesting.'

Pleased not to hear of any on-set dramas in Malta, Snyder wanted to capitalise on the presumed success *Gladiator* would bring. His reasoning was that you don't win an Oscar for just one film; you need to have some other solid performances to showcase as well. He felt that with *Yards* coming out, one more great film should do the trick.

A script called *Quills* (2000) was doing the rounds, and Snyder thought it was one of the best ones he had read in years. He quickly got in touch with the producers, desperate to see if the part of Coulmier was available. Typically, Jude Law was once again linked to a role that Snyder wanted for Phoenix.

However, one of the producers on *The Yards* happened to be working on *Quills* – but he refused to believe that the studio would accept Phoenix in the role. Snyder insisted that if the studio got a screen test, the producer wouldn't block the test. The head of casting at the studio insisted that while they loved Phoenix they just didn't think he was right for the role.

Snyder persevered and was told they had another film in mind for Joaquin and the director was desperate to get him – so Snyder worked out a deal whereby Phoenix would meet the director if he could get a screen test for the role.

Phoenix had read the script by Doug Wright and fallen in love with it, calling it 'extraordinary'. He had heard that actors like Geoffrey Rush and Kate Winslet were attached to the project and didn't think he had a chance of getting a part. He was three months into shooting *Gladiator* when his agency team told him that there was a chance of meeting director Philip Kaufman for the project. He would have to fly to London, however, to which Phoenix responded 'Absofuckinglutely.'

Trying to get Joaquin to London was hectic because of his shooting on Gladiator, and Joaquin was less than thrilled to audition while he was deep into the character of Commodus. Snyder had a sneaking suspicion that the deal was made with the casting boss because she thought there was no way he would be able to get time off from *Gladiator*. However, they managed to work things out.

Phoenix later said, 'Then I didn't hear anything, which was fine because I was so wrapped up in *Gladiator*. One day I was between scenes and my mom called and told me I got the part. Suddenly I was ten years old, and it was my first job – and I had beat out what seemed like the whole world.'

While Joaquin would have loved to have time off between films, he would have to shoot *Gladiator*, extensive re-shoots on *The Yards* and *Quills* pretty much back-to-back. He started having second thoughts about *Quills*. He was exhausted, and couldn't think of anything worse than appearing in front of the camera so soon after *Gladiator*.

The Burton Agency feared the worst – was Joaquin showing similar signs and strains to those of his older brother? Thinking back, he hadn't been right all that year. Calls weren't returned for up to a week, he was mumbling and incoherent more than usual. It was decided that Iris and Chris would phone Heart, who in return, after listening to them for an hour, decided to speak to Joaquin.

With Iris in tow, Heart agreed to keep Joaquin company – with his sisters also paying a visit. Snyder said, 'It was really a hard shoot for him for some reason, and in fact it was a very hard year. Joaquin and River were not the sort of people that can go from film to film. They put their heart and soul into a project. That wasn't planned. It just happened.

'When you see a script like *Quills* you can't let that one go, and I worked really hard for that. He was just really tired. They were really emotional roles. An actor knows that things are going to change after these films and he was probably thinking of what that would entail. He was always under the radar at that point. There was a lot of pressure put upon him and there was going to be more, and I think he knew that.'

Joaquin said, 'I shot them [*Gladiator*, *The Yards* and *Quills*] all over a year and a half [1998–99], and with *Quills*, because we shot in order it became more and more intense as the shoot went on, and my character kind of disintegrates. So when I finished that film, I was exhausted.

'I went straight home to my mom's. I sat in bed for, like, six weeks and did absolutely nothing.'

CHAPTER SEVEN

THE MOVIE STAR

Joaquin would brand *Quills* 'as one of my toughest shoots'.

'I'd finished and I went and did re-shoots on *The Yards* for a week, came back to London and started rehearsals for *Quills*. I was exhausted. We shot virtually in order; some of the most intense scenes were in those last weeks. The last three weeks on *Quills*. I didn't know if I could make it through the day. But Geoffrey Rush would come in, or Kate Winslet, and inspire you. It's a joint effort; you need everyone around you.'

Joaquin added, 'I knew going into *Quills* that it would be risky and that was part of the attraction and

I guess I've always kind of done that because maybe it's real simple, maybe it's just boring to play it safe.'

Doug Wright raved about Joaquin's performance to *GQ* magazine: 'He had a cigarette dangling out of his mouth and he had on these really intense aviator shades and his hair was all tousled, and he was like, "Hey, dude". Then he walked onto the sound stage, and the cigarette gets stamped out and the glasses come off and someone runs a comb through his hair, and the guy is suddenly an early-nineteenth-century priest. It was the most transformative moment – it took my breath away. Joaquin is someone who could slide by you in the hallway, but aim a lens at him and he becomes thirty feet tall.'

The adaptation of Doug Wright's award-winning play focused on the Marquis de Sade's last years in an insane asylum. Joaquin played the Abbé du Coulmier – the man who would oversee De Sade's confinement.

Talking about his character, Joaquin said, 'I think that he loves him as you love the most difficult child in the world. My character, Coulmier, is one of those people that can find the best in each person and wants to draw that out of them. It's a love-hate relationship. It's very difficult. How do you deal with someone who is so antagonistic? Coulmier is a very rational and logical man. The realisation at the end of the film is that the

Marquis denies his ability to love, and Coulmier denies his sexual feelings.

'I'm totally not familiar with his [the Marquis's] work. I started to read some, and then I felt I didn't want to be that familiar with it. It was important to maintain what world we were in. This is not historically accurate. For instance, Madeleine was a prostitute; her mother would prostitute her to the Marquis. Coulmier was a four-foot hunchback with a bum leg. That was the one part that I felt was really accurate, and typecasting!' (Pleather, a synthetic plastic 'leather' fabric would be used for his shoes to accommodate Joaquin's veganisim.)

Indeed, the film would come under fire from historical experts, citing inaccuracies and simplifying his life. However, Doug insisted that this was a re-imagining of De Sade's time in the asylum.

The New York Times stated, 'Mr. Phoenix's thoughtful performance makes it clear that Coulmier clings to decency because it offers him self-definition and sanity; without it, he'd be lost, potentially worse off than any of the asylum's inmates.'

While online magazine *Salon* noted, 'Phoenix's Abbé radiates so much purity and goodness that he invites us to laugh at him: Going around the asylum's art room, he stops at one inmate's florid, flaming painting and notes encouragingly, "It's far better to paint fires than to set them, isn't it?" But before long he's less a comical figure than a tragic prisoner himself. Even the set of his shoulders, girlishly narrow-looking in a fitted cassock, suggests a man who doesn't dare face up to his own decidedly masculine passions.

'His scenes with Winslet's Madeleine have a shapely delicacy: The two of them are almost girlish together, but Phoenix never lets us lose sight of the Abbé's repressed desire. Sade's virility is a gaudy music-hall show; the Abbé's is more muted but no less genuine.'

Phoenix's stock looked certain to rocket, with *Premiere* magazine saying, 'Joaquin Phoenix is quite the conquering hero in casting circles. Not only did he beat British beauty Jude Law for *Gladiator*, but he also vanquished Law, Billy Crudup and Guy Pearce for the young-priest-in-love role opposite Kate Winslet in November's *Quills*. And with Phoenix's performance in James Gray's *The Yards* already getting critical praise this year at the Cannes film festival, it looks like Phoenix will have three performances with potential Oscar buzz this year.'

He was indeed Oscar nominated for his *Gladiator* role, but would lose out to Benicio del Toro's performance in *Traffic*.

The release of *Gladiator* was supposed to herald the

arrival of two movie stars – Russell Crowe and Joaquin Phoenix. Both were already made – Crowe had worked extensively for years, while Phoenix had enough experience with his brother to know what was coming if the film was ultimately the success it turned out to be. However, it was clear who was the more suited to it. Crowe's brash manner and seeming desire for perfection would rankle, but it's obvious he had the self-confidence to handle being an A-list star.

Phoenix lacked this confidence and drive.

Nielsen would say, 'He fretted all the time', while Crowe hopes 'he learns one day how good he is because he's a damn fine actor.' He reminded Harris of a young Marlon Brando, recalling a story of how Brando was nervous, fluffing his lines during rehearsals of *A Streetcar Named Desire* but would turn out amazing performances in front on an audience. Harris would say after the film was released, 'Joaquin doesn't believe he's good and you have to tell him how fucking marvellous he is. He says, "I'm hopeless, they all think I'm as good as River, I shouldn't be in this picture, I should be selling cars, I'm not an actor at all."'

Harris took special interest in Joaquin, after working with his brother on 1994's *Silent Tongue*. The unlikely pair would bond during the shoot, with Harris saying, 'He [River] looked upon me as a kind of a father figure.

He'd knock at my door, ask if he could come in and sleep. He'd fucking sleep on the couch. I could hear him rehearsing his lines at four in the morning. I said, "Fucking, go to sleep." He'd be in the bathroom, taking a crap, doing his lines.'

A *GQ* cover interview, which was to cement his status as a movie-star-in-waiting reflected not only Phoenix's inability to seize on his fame, but just how easily his colleagues and friends would paint him as a quirky and somewhat unstable actor. While Ridley Scott would say, 'Whatever happens to Joaquin on film, I always feel sorry for him. He's kind of a wounded individual,' Wright would add, 'Joaquin is genuine, with access to absolutely volcanic emotional places in his soul.' Affleck would back up Phoenix's assertion that he would be viewed with suspicion when boarding a plane ('They never think I belong in First Class') admitting, 'I've been on planes with him, and I don't really want to look at him, because he sits down and drinks sixteen shots of whatever he can find and pulls his shirt over his head and stays like that for the rest of the flight.'

On one hand it painted him as unique and just a little bit dangerous compared to the other pampered movie stars, but to Iris Burton and her agency it proved a damning article in terms of them flogging their star to

Above: Phoenix appeared alongside Robert Duvall in crime drama, *We Own the Night* (2007).

Below: Phoenix sits alongside Mark Ruffalo during a press conference for *Reservation Road* (2007).

Top left: Phoenix and Affleck during the announcement of the former's 'retirement' from acting.

Top right: A shady looking Joaquin stands next to Casey Affleck during a children's benefit performance in 2008.

Below: Phoenix made his shock announcement to 'retire' during the promotion for *Two Lovers* in 2008. He appeared in his 'final film' alongside Vinessa Shaw (pictured) and Gwyneth Paltrow.

During his hiatus from acting, Phoenix enlisted the help of rap
producer P. Diddy (*top*) and hung-out with hip-hop artist and actor
Jamie Foxx (*below*).

Phoenix's career move was met mild amusement within the industry.
Giada Colagrande and Willem Dafoe (*top left*) lampooned the actor-
turned-rap-star following his infamous appearance on Letterman;
Ben Stiller (*top right*), who appeared in *I'm Still Here* pitching his film
Greenberg to an incomprehensible Phoenix, appeared at the 2009 Oscar
ceremony replete with Joaquin-style beard alongside Natalie Portman.
Phoenix ignored the detractors, however, and continued to promote
Two Lovers along with his co-stars Gwyneth Paltrow and Vinessa Shaw.

Phoenix performed live on numerous occasions during his stint as a rapper in 2009. He is pictured here on stage in a Miami Beach club, just prior to launching an expletive filled rant at a heckler. Casey Affleck can be seen in the background filming the whole incident (*below*).

Over a year after his extraordinary interview on *The Late Show with David Letterman*, Phoenix made another appearance on the same show in September 2010 to explain what was behind his shock 'career move'.

the studios. Aided by a less-than-impressive interview on *The Tonight Show*, the way they saw it was that just one week had ruined years of hard work. Referring to the interviews, Burton would tell Snyder, 'What the fuck were these people thinking? They've fucking ruined my chances of making money. I can't believe James Gray…and what the fuck was Casey thinking?'

A UK journalist, who didn't want to be named, recalls meeting Phoenix for the *Gladiator* press junket: '[It was] in Rome. Spring 2000, I think. He was a polite guy, but I remember him being really nervous. Quite jittery. I don't think it was for any other reason than he really didn't like taking part in the media circus. In fact, when we talked a bit about what makes him uncomfortable, he quite openly said "this fucking junket", though in a jokey way, not in any way angry.

'But he was a nice guy, although he got quite upset when I suggested his character was evil. The baddie. I mean, he admitted that obviously Commodus is the villain of the piece, but was very quick to point out that there was a reason behind the character's malice, the whole ignored by his father thing. He really seemed to hate the idea that I misunderstood his character. Whether that was because he thought I was an idiot, or whether he was worried that people would misinterpret his performance, or even that his performance hadn't done what it was supposed to have done, well, I've thought all of them were true at some point.'

He continued, 'I remember him smoking and being fidgety. He didn't like journalists even then, but I think he realised with something like *Gladiator* that he'd have to put up with them because it was this big behemoth of a movie.'

Snyder would say, 'That article had Ridley and the director of *The Yards* come out with derogatory comments about working with him. And I thought, "Oh, this is not really good. It came out just after *Gladiator* – it put a dampener on things."

'Even after *Gladiator* opened and it made so much money it was still hard to get him work. There were still five people ahead of him that would get those scripts. They all had to pass. In 2001 those projects were less than in 1993. It was hard.'

He would still be offered some roles, though, and was in talks for *Pearl Harbor*.

'Yes, I had a meeting with Michael Bay about *Pearl Harbor*. I thought it was a well-written script but ultimately it just wasn't a film I really wanted to make. It all worked out well, though, because they ended up casting Josh Hartnett, who's a really sweet kid. I think it will be great for him.'

Talking about blockbusters, he told the media, 'I

would do one of those huge movies because I want to experience it. I think it's probably a lot easier for me to do a scene in which I'm having an intimate conversation with someone on a quiet little set than it is to scream at a blue screen because I think a giant dragon's penis is trying to swallow me. That, to me, is going to be a challenge.'

He was asked to play Wolverine in the first *X-Men* movie after the film's original choice, Dougray Scott, pulled out. Because he was a comic-book fan, he gave it serious thought, but ultimately passed on the opportunity. He was also wanted for an adaptation of the Anne Rice novel *Queen of the Damned*, the third in *The Vampire Chronicles*' series, but the agency thought it would be a bit unnerving because of the obvious ties to River.

It seemed Joaquin was a becoming a huge fish in a small pond at the agency. He had had the red carpet rolled out in front of him. The bigger agents were circling and Joaquin suddenly dropped the bombshell – he felt he didn't need to audition anymore, the irony being that the reason he got the *Gladiator* part was because Jude Law demanded the same perk. It wasn't long after that Joaquin would tell Iris that he wanted to leave the Burton Agency – and instead would begin negotiations elsewhere, eventually deciding on CAA.

First off, however, he plumped for *Buffalo Soldiers* (2001), which would be overseen by the Burton Agency. An anarchic black comedy in the vein of *M*A*S*H*, Phoenix plays a loveable rogue who chooses military service rather than go to jail over car-theft charges. It was a popular option in the late 1980s – which is when the film is set.

Stationed in Stuttgart, Phoenix had a ball playing Elwood, who makes money on the side by selling army supplies to the German black market. Throw in having an affair with a military official's wife and daughter, as well as selling heroin, and you can see why – especially post 9/11 – the film's studio began to have worries once the film was completed.

'But there was no intention to offend or criticise,' said Joaquin. 'I always saw this movie as being about human nature. It's not a critique of Americans or the military; it's about man's inherent desire to fight. It's that Nietzsche quote at the end, that there's always some war somewhere with someone. (The actual quote is: 'When there is peace the warlike man attacks himself'.)

'I thought it was refreshing to have a protagonist that was an antihero, for a change. You see so many earnest characters in movies all the time; everyone has a purpose. But Elwood – there's nothing that even makes him obviously likeable. He really doesn't care about much. He has a kind of street Zen about him, which I like. A fuck-it-who-cares attitude!'

Screenwriter Eric Axel Weiss said, 'I find that one thing that I love when reading a novel – whether it's the character, tone, setting, etc. – and *that* is what I always want to somehow preserve in my script. In the case of *Buffalo Soldiers* I loved the black comic tone, so I wanted to keep it. For me, that was the spirit of the book. And I also loved the big heroin cook-off at the climax of the novel. Gotta have a great ending! Everything else was up for grabs.'

Discussing the way he put the script together, he said, 'First, I read the novel (by Robert O'Connor) several times over, noting bits of dialogue I liked or set pieces that would be cool to put in the script. There was a lot of stuff that I liked but if it couldn't serve my story, then it was out.

'A novel, especially a good one like *Buffalo Soldiers*, takes full advantage of its medium and tells a story very differently than a narrative feature film. When you're reading *Buffalo Soldiers* the novel, you get this feeling of momentum. It's a real page-turner. But when I outlined the action of the book, it just seemed like reflection, observation and episodic events. So, using the same characters and general situation of the novel, I created a new through-line for the movie. Elwood stealing the weapons, selling them to the Turk, trying to get out of the weapons deal after his buddy dies and then forced to go through with it – none of that is in the novel.'

It would feature a wonderfully charming performance by Phoenix. But although the film was released in Canada in 2001, it wasn't released in the UK until 2002, and in America the year after that because of post 9/11 sensitivity concerns. It was always going to rankle right-wing commentators. Even the poster drew criticism – with many of the pro-war sector angry at a handsome Phoenix flashing a peace sign, with a tag line that read, 'Steal All That You Can Steal'. The reaction was fierce, and Miramax decided to re-shoot the poster.

However, when reports of the poster re-shoot surfaced another row broke out. A source told entertainment website Contactmusic.com: 'People were outraged that a peace sign had turned into something obscene that should be banned. Some people were also outraged with what they saw as a squelching of first-amendment rights.'

A spokesperson for Miramax replied, 'We heard from people who were both for and against the poster. And while we respect the opinions of both parties, we've decided to let Joaquin flash his peace sign.'

Army spokeswoman Kathleen Canham Ross said before the film's release, 'We did not support *Buffalo Soldiers*. From what I have read, it isn't a movie that we would particularly care to have the United States military's name associated with.'

Director Gregor Jordan would hit out at the critics, saying, 'In the UK, no one gets upset, but in America, where the President is fighting these military campaigns in the name of democracy, the first casualty seems to be freedom of speech, the cornerstone of any democracy.'

Weiss would add, 'The film was written and produced pre-9/11. I remember getting a phone call from the producers shortly after the film premiered in Toronto. They were tremendously excited because they just sold the movie to Miramax. That was September 10, 2001. When 9/11 happened, I was surprised *Buffalo Soldiers* was deemed controversial. While it does deal with the idea that war will always be with us, I don't see it as anti-military, and it's not like it's a comedy about hijacking. But I guess some see it as "unpatriotic".'

The *Guardian*'s Peter Bradshaw wrote, 'An acrid and deliciously unpleasant satire on the US military in the tradition of M*A*S*H and *Catch-22*, directed by the Australian Gregor Jordan, soon also to present his version of the Ned Kelly story. This film was actually made in 2001, but held over in the aftermath of 9/11, and that's not altogether surprising, given its magnificent lack of respect for the American army and US of A values in general.

'Joaquin Phoenix gives a very funny performance as Elwood.'

Following on from the relative failure of *Buffalo Soldiers* ('It was a great film though,' said Snyder. 'It just wasn't marketed well.'), his new agency team landed him a part in M. Night Shyamalan's eagerly awaited alien invasion thriller *Signs* (2002).

He had a meal with the director to talk about the part, who came up with the idea for the film during post-production work on his previous film *Unbreakable*. 'He described it at first,' he told Phoenix, 'how it is the appearance of crop circles on the family farm. And then as I read the script, the metaphor became clear to me. That's kind of Night's expertise in a way...he brings you these authentic characters and yet they have these amazing epiphanies about themselves and the world but it's something with which everyone can identify.'

It was a plum role for Phoenix, who would play the minor-league baseball player brother of Mel Gibson's former priest – a man who is still distraught by the death of his wife. Raising his kids at his farmyard home, he is stunned to discover strange crop circles outside.

Executive producer Kathleen Kennedy said in the press material, 'There's been speculation as to whether these (crop) signs were done by some prankster or were in fact a sign from outer space. And that was Night's original concept – to combine that with a character who is clearly facing demons.

'Night always tells stories that have entertainment value to them. This is scary and suspenseful, and has an aspect to it that makes people want to see the movie, because they know that they are going to have a good time. On the other hand, what Night so successfully does is he always has a subtext to his stories and this is about a man regaining his faith.'

Bruce Willis had been cast as the lead in Shyamalan's previous two movies – *Sixth Sense* and *Unbreakable*. But this time he turned to another eighties action star – Mel Gibson. Explaining his casting process, he said, 'Actors have to believe in the screenplay. That sounds silly, but people can be doing it for a pay cheque or whatever it is, but not necessarily because they believe in the storytelling and the story that's being told. And until I see that look in the actor's eyes like, I got this, I would do this for nothing, I can't give them the part.'

Said Gibson, 'It's not something that you come to the

realisation of straight away because it's constructed very nicely. There is a lot of mystery involved, and that of course makes you want to look further. It keeps you in long enough, until pieces start to come together and you start to understand the characters in stages, which is great, because in real life you normally learn about people in bits and pieces. There was something very real about it. And it was the kind of project I hadn't done before.'

He added, 'It's a film about spirituality and belief and faith. Graham is an Episcopalian minister who seems very insistent and stubbornly opposed to the idea of anyone calling him Father. And you soon realise that he is someone who has serious doubts. He has been shut down by a devastating life experience. It's not clear at the beginning of the film what has happened, but you sense it from his behaviour and you find out the exact nature of his wounds as the story unfolds.'

Producer Frank Marshall would note, 'I think it's the kind of part that all actors are looking for. It has a tremendous arc – a character who loses his faith and gets it back. And it gives audiences a chance to see yet another side of Mel Gibson, who's already shown his comedic side, his action side, his dramatic side.'

And on the making of a film, 'I make the movie visually before we make the movie. It's important to me that I understand the movie before any actor comes to me...that I understand its nature. And so when we get on set, and are setting up for a shot, I know where I am going to use it and we don't have any extra stuff. I don't have to have an actor do a great performance in a shot we won't use.

'A lot of the discipline in filmmaking has been lost now because of computer editing and the way we do things now. It's so, "Figure it out later. Why spend the time to do it now?" I want to create an environment where people can risk themselves because they feel so safe that what they are doing is going to be used to its fullest extent.'

Phoenix would note, 'He doesn't ever lose the emotional core of the characters, which is a difficult balance. If you are very technical, and it becomes about how the camera moves, or the lighting, you are in danger of losing that humanistic quality...or vice versa and you pay attention to only that, the technical side could suffer. Yet he somehow manages to do it all. And it creates this wonderful atmosphere on set that is very inspiring as an actor.'

It was an atmosphere that was heightened by serial practical joker Mel Gibson. Phoenix told Associated Press, 'When I did *Signs* with Mel Gibson he played this big practical joke on me on set. There's this long, tense scene where I'm watching TV alone in a closet, and when we were filming it suddenly got very quiet. After a while I realised everyone had left the set and I was still sitting there, locked in this closet on my own. I was in there shouting, "Hey Guys! What's going on?"

'This went on for about twenty minutes. I refused to leave in the end. I didn't want to give them the satisfaction, so I just sat there. I'll get him back though.

'It's kind of embarrassing, but I did jump a few times. I was pretty scared. And I laughed. I think Mel is so funny.'

Critics weren't bowled over by the film, with many praising the director's obvious visual skills, but feeling that he was going over the same old ground.

Time Out stated, 'Shyamalan is technically a superb film-maker, for all that he's picked up most of his tricks from Spielberg and Hitchcock. The teasing first hour or so tingles with eerie suggestion and ominous disquiet. The film gets darker as the weight of what's transpiring hits home. The climax is pure horror – basement black. Of course, they blow it, big time. The denouement's an embarrassment and you hate yourself for being sucked in.'

While the *Guardian*'s film critic wrote, 'Shyamalan has directed a film without the novelty and ingenuity of his first two. What is left is a derivative, underpowered picture. This talented and, at thirty two, very young director must now find new ideas – maybe working with someone else's scripts. Because his film-making identity is in danger of fading.'

Nevertheless, it was an enjoyable shooting experience for Joaquin and he would team up again with the director for the follow-up – *The Village* (2004).

He said tellingly, 'So we had shorthand that we had developed on *Signs*, but to be honest with you, there is something kind of intimidating about that. Part of what's good about working with someone that you've never worked with before is they don't really know you as well, and are getting to know a character; they can't tell the difference between what's you and what's the character and what's happening. After *Signs* we got to know each other better, so he was able to tell when I was bullshitting and that's well, that's mutual, and so that was a little intimidating.'

Joaquin was paid $1 million for *Signs*, but was said to have been given a $4 million pay rise for *The Village*.

In the press notes, the plot is described as thus: 'In *The Village* the elders of the town have made a choice to coexist with their community inside an isolated village. Cutting themselves off from the rest of the world, their fear of the creatures, and what other evils may exist beyond their town borders, gives them motivation to stay intact and safe with their loved ones.

'We can't ignore fear. We live with fear every day. Whether it be creatures in the woods, or in our modern society, the uncertainty of the safety of our own children the moment they leave the house to go to school. Fear surrounds us daily as we watch the network news and hear of child abductions, enemies of war, or terrorism. In the words of Franklin D. Roosevelt, is it true that "The only thing we have to fear is fear itself"? Or does society show us otherwise?

'What do we do to maintain our sense of community in times of fear? The people of *The Village* bonded together and went to great lengths to keep their community safe and protect themselves from their fears.'

Playing on the fear and paranoia that surrounded the events of 9/11, Shyamalan would say, 'In our contemporary world I often ask myself how far would I go to protect my children? Would I move to a farm in the middle of nowhere and live like the people of *The Village*? We like to believe we would, but how many of us have? What sacrifices are we truly making to better our situation?

'Fear doesn't necessarily need to be something we are afraid of. Sometimes it just lets our imaginations run wild. I hope through *The Village*, audiences are able to explore a world of fear and how, even in the midst of chaos, you can find a way to cope.'

While writing the script, Night wrote the part of Lucius with Joaquin in mind, and was then delighted that he agreed to work with him again. Phoenix said, 'I really enjoy reading Night's scripts and talking to him in depth about the story. He knows his characters so well and even if something is not on the page, he knows the history of every single character and shares it with you.

'Lucius is rebellious but in a quiet kind of way, because of the way he has been raised. When the story of *The Village* begins it is the starting point of Lucius's journey on his own, and with Ivy. Like all the characters in the story he is richly unique, but also fully realised.'

Joining Joaquin would be newcomer Bryce Dallas Howard – daughter of Joaquin's *Parenthood* director Ron. Night had seen her in an off-Broadway play and immediately met up with her afterwards, inviting her for lunch and giving her the script.

'This is the first time film audiences will see Bryce. You are going to think she is Ivy. This character is going to be her. After casting Bryce everything fell into place. It was so clear who else should be on board. There were so many layers to it.'

Bryce added, 'I am so grateful that Night had this amount of faith to cast an unknown actress like myself in this beautiful love story. This unbelievably potent love story of Ivy and Lucius is a love that I think everyone should strive to have.

'Night works with such generosity and lets the actor work freely within the canvas he has created. I think he gives this same gift to the audience, a chance for them to intelligently manipulate and interpret the story. He assumes the audience's imaginations are vivid and that they are starved for a challenging and complicated story.'

Shyamalan told the actors before they were cast that they would have to undergo a boot camp if they wanted to be in the film. 'I wanted to form a real community of people where they needed to rely on one another for survival. I didn't just want to do my version of this movie. I wanted to be surprised. I wanted to be entertained. I wanted to come to work and not know what was going to happen, and the only way that is going to happen is if the actors are in it with me, standing right beside me.'

They would undertake rural training, while living on farms and, with two names being drawn out of a hat every evening, would prepare and make food for everyone that night. The same care and preparation on getting the realism just right would go on the costumes as well.

Oscar-winning costume designer Ann Roth said, 'I wanted the clothes in *The Village* to be a non-event, and I mean that in the most positive way. The costumes had to simply look as if the townspeople had made the clothes themselves. They didn't have access to fine laces or European textiles. That was a hard task to achieve.'

One of the film's stars, Sigourney Weaver, recalled her experiences on the nineteenth-century style boot camp: 'We had a week where we were living in Philadelphia and going to different historical farms and leaning how to plow and how to hew a log and how to shock corn.

'We made meals for each other. Then we moved into a girl-scout camp for two weeks, and we had a lot of activities, and also rehearsed. We did some work. We met with Night in the afternoon. We got up each morning and had to make a fire from scratch. It took me about three days. Everybody would've starved if they were in my group and then we ended up living in this bed-and-breakfast for three months. That could have been like a horrible reality show, actors jumping out of the windows to get away from each other. But it was actually really fun.'

Joaquin added, 'It was good. I mean it was really just an opportunity for us to focus on the film, to not have any other distractions and to get to know each other, and to think in character and to develop our relationships, in character, which is important.

'Oftentimes, it depends on the actors. There are some actors that really embrace trying to look inside the part and then there are others that are on the phones all the time. So just to get all of those actors together in an isolated environment, it's really beneficial, at least that's what I found.'

Released in 2004, unfortunately the film was largely slated by the critics. The negativity surrounding the film came earlier than the release. A shooting script was leaked online, with many suggesting that, because of the clumsy grammar, bad spelling and an overall poor story, it was fake. However, after it was claimed to be the real deal, Aintitcoolnews wrote, 'This can't be it. He's putting together a good cast so far, filled with character actors like Adrien Brody and Brendan Gleeson and Judy Greer and Joaquin Phoenix and Sigourney Weaver and William Hurt and Michael Pitt and Cherry Jones, and he wouldn't sign all those people to do a third-rate community theatre version of *The Crucible* filled with cornball dialogue and stiff characters that are more type than anything else. Nobody's drawn convincingly. Not Lucius Hunt (Phoenix), the shy and introverted young man who wants to challenge the traditional teachings of his village elders...'

The website went on to add, 'There is no way Disney is going to bet on *The Woods* [working title] as their big summer movie if the script is built on a two page twist ending so cheap and ridiculous that it would have been laughed out of a pitch meeting at the most obnoxious of the dozens of direct-to-syndication *Twilight Zone/Outer Limit* rip-offs on TV over the years. There is no way the punchline to the new M. Night Shyamalan film is some guy shaking his head and saying, "Crazy fucking white people", before getting in a truck and driving away. I refuse to believe it.'

That final line spread like wildfire on the internet, with it becoming something of an in-joke in the online film community. The scene was eventually shot with different dialogue.

Esteemed critic Roger Ebert wrote, '*The Village* is a colossal miscalculation, a movie based on a premise that cannot support it, a premise so transparent it would be laughable were the movie not so deadly solemn... To call the ending an anticlimax would be an insult not only to climax but to prefixes. It's a crummy secret, about one step up the ladder of narrative originality from "It was all a dream". It's so witless, in fact, that when we do discover the secret, we want to rewind the film so we don't know the secret anymore.'

It still performed solidly in the box office, however. But Joaquin needed to land more leading-man parts. One role that would define him to a worldwide audience was just around the corner, but he would be lucky to get the part if he didn't align himself to more studio films.

CHAPTER EIGHT

STEP UP THE LADDER

Joaquin Phoenix was beginning to play the game. 'At times in my life I've been aware of certain kinds of strategies. You can't deny the business aspect of film-making; it would be totally naïve to do so. I've never let it dictate my choices, but I've been aware of it, and have done films that I felt I needed to do. For instance, I thought *Ladder 49* had the potential to tell an important story and I thought we could do it authentically.

'But I also knew that I needed to play a lead in a studio film at that point, so I knew it was important for me to take that on. I had offers for leads in other studio films but I didn't do them. You have to be aware of that. Part of the reason I was able to play Johnny Cash was because I was in *Signs* and it made a lot of money. I think Jim Mangold would have wanted me for the role anyway, but I don't think the studio would have okayed it otherwise. So that's what you have to balance out in your career.'

However, interviews were still a problem. He is quoted as saying, 'I think the day that I become comfortable doing interviews and going on talk shows is the day that I don't know what it is to be a human being anymore. I'm quite comfortable and not awkward in my life, but when I do press I can be awkward, because I don't enjoy it. I don't like the attention. I was really naive about what's involved in the film industry. I've been acting since I was eight, and I never looked at entertainment magazines, never watched entertainment shows. I don't think one should be comfortable standing on a stage with people applauding and laughing at every stupid thing you say.'

He added, 'It's one thing in a normal situation, when they genuinely like something you said, but when you're with an audience that seems to be trained to applaud at any given moment, it's hard to be really satisfied. It's a fake orgasm.'

In between his M. Night Shyamalan roles, Phoenix would star in two films. One was animated caper *Brother Bear*, where he would play the character of

Kenai – a brash man who finds himself transformed into a grizzly bear.

Producer Chuck Williams recalls, 'It's basically an original story. Aaron and I started from scratch by reading a lot of Native American myths and transformation stories. We discovered that practically every culture around the world had some kind of story about people transforming into animals. Many of them were about boys changing into bears as a coming-of-age ritual. Some of the stories even had humans pretending to be bears for a period of time and then they'd come out and be considered men of the tribe. Our original idea was a father-son story about a rebellious son who was changed into a bear and had to make amends with his father in order to change back.'

Director Aaron Blaise added, 'The transformation myths were designed to teach life lessons and that's why they were passed down all these years by different cultures. They're structured in ways that are unlike Western storytelling, with the idea that you could go from one culture to another, meaning one animal world to the human world. They felt that the animals were just people in different clothing. We thought it was a cool idea that you could cross over from one culture to another.'

He also worked on indie sci-fi drama *It's All About*

Love. It was much maligned by critics. However, *The Village Voice* didn't agree, claiming, '*It's All About Love* is, by any measure, a colossal folly – ridiculed at its Sundance '03 premiere (where, to this viewer at least, it seemed like a lone beacon of nutty integrity), supposedly disowned by its stars (rumour has it Claire Danes burst into tears upon seeing the end result) and jettisoned by original distributor Focus. But this $10-million Danish-British-French-US-Japanese-Swedish-Norwegian-German-Dutch co-production is a film *maudit* for the ages – rapturous and inexplicable in equal measure.'

Phoenix was still looking for that big leading-man role, and he would find what he was looking for in *Ladder 49*.

The press notes began by posing the question, 'What does it take to be the man who runs headlong into a burning building when everyone else is trying to get out? *Ladder 49* is a moving look at how extra-ordinary heroes emerge out of ordinary lives, relationships and dreams.'

The film focuses on a young devoted firefighter, Jack, played by Joaquin. Trapped in a burning building and cut off from help, he looks back at his life and the decisions he has made. (Ironically, during an interview in 1995, Joaquin told a journalist while watching a fire engine speed by, 'Aren't firemen beautiful? Every time I see a fire truck or ambulance drive by I blow them a kiss. I think what they're doing is so beautiful'.)

Said director Jay Russell, 'The idea for me was that the audience would learn more and more as Jack learns more and more – and hopefully, they would be drawn not only into the excitement and heroism of his life, but the heartbreak and personal dilemmas of it as well. I think we are all fascinated by how people live with the knowledge that every single day might be their last. It's a question we all have to face but fireman are an inspiration because they really live it.'

Producer Casey Silver said, 'I wanted to make a fire-fighting movie in an unsentimental, honest way that would celebrate the dignity and nobility of these guys. I was thinking of a film that would, at its core, be about characters and human emotions, but at the same time would capture the dramatic spectacle and suspense of fire-fighting.'

With this in mind he took the idea to screenwriter Lewis Colick. 'I told Lewis I wanted to explore firefighters from an entirely new angle, not from the usual thriller or adventure perspective, but instead taking a very truthful, no-holds-barred view into their world. I asked him to go as far into the firefighters' reality as possible and to focus on their families – not just on the wives who simply kiss their men goodbye, but as a central part of their lives, ambitions and motivation. The idea was to give a real sense of these two powerful families that sustain firefighters – their brothers on the job and their wives and children at home.'

After meeting with a real fireman, Colick added, 'With Jack, I wanted to create a guy who would be symbolic of a certain kind of fireman I got to know – a good-hearted family man who loves his friends, loves his wife, but when that bell rings is ready to risk it all, no matter what, to save somebody he doesn't even know.

'Creating Jack gave me a chance to reveal what a fireman's life is really like. Because a lot of it is just waiting around for a fire, playing games, pulling pranks, shooting the breeze, but then it's punctuated by these highly dramatic events that can change other people's lives and affect you forever.

'I thought having Jack look back on his life would give us a chance to tell a lot of the great stories I heard about of life-altering fires and near-miraculous rescues. It was also a chance to have him look back at why he became a fireman in the first place, what it means to him, and most of all, how he has managed to juxtapose the incredible risk of a deadly job with his family-centred personal life.'

He added, 'I honestly believe that a lot of these guys are just born or raised a certain way that give them this an unshakeable feeling that they just want to do good in this world. It's an inspiring thing to see first-hand. At the same time, they're also husbands and dads and buddies just like the rest of us. They're definitely not sombre people who sit around being grave and serious, they love to have a good time and they also make mistakes and have very typical problems.

'They love to have a good time and party and spend time just being with their families. I wanted to get across some of their fun spirit, some of their difficulties dealing with the pressure of the job, but also show that when the bell rings, everything changes for these guys and they become life-savers.'

Director Jay Russell was reading scripts late at night, hoping to find something that would resonate. Known for films like *My Dog Skip* and his documentary work, he eventually stumbled on a script for *Ladder 49*.

He would stay up half the night reading the script, determined to read through it all. 'I was really moved. I was touched not only by the subject matter but especially by the lives of these characters who you come to know and who really mean something to you by the end.'

Right then, Russell determined that he wanted to

make the movie – and that he wanted to do so with a distinctly emotional and intimate style not usually seen in fire-fighting movies. 'I really wanted to bring these characters to life and I wanted to take the audience into authentic fires like they've never been taken into fire before. I wanted to capture not just the look of a fire, but the intensity, the fear and the amazing things the people do to battle them and save innocent civilians.'

Written before 9/11, the script was originally set in New York, and while Russell acknowledges that the tragic events possibly sped up the film being green-lit by studio bosses, it 'had nothing to do with us'.

However, Russell agreed to direct it – on one condition. 'I'd lived in New York for 11 years and would love to shoot a movie in New York, but this wasn't going to be the one,' he explained. 'If the movie takes place in New York it becomes about that one day. The whole point of the movie is that while it's absolutely a tribute to the firefighters on 9/11, it's also a tribute to the firefighters on 9/10, 9/12 and 9/13.'

The role of Jack Morrison is key to the whole movie. Russell cast Phoenix, because, 'I've always admired Joaquin, especially the way he seems to be able to just disappear into a role. And I knew that's what he would do with Jack Morrison. He embodied this role from the inside out, capturing the soul of Jack first and then his physicality. He also commits like no one else I've ever met. He spent months and months training for this movie – not so that he could *look* like a firefighter, but so that he could essentially *become* a full-fledged firefighter. You really see the effect of everything he went through for this role in his face and his performance.'

In the press notes, Silver added, 'Joaquin was passionate about this material and felt a real sense of obligation to get it right. Joaquin just doesn't know how to do things in a false way. He brings to the character of Jack Morrison an authenticity and emotional truthfulness that carry the humour, the meaning and the poignancy of the story home. Perhaps he was an unconventional choice, but he was the right choice for this film.'

Phoenix said, 'We all have heard about the special bond between firefighters, but until I read this script, I didn't really think about how deeply those bonds extend beyond the job. I didn't know how their lives at work intertwine with their family lives. And that's what I loved about the script. To me, it's very much about family. It's about Jack finding his role in two different families that he is equally passionate about – the fire-fighting family and his real family at home – even though they are often in conflict.'

He continues, 'I was impressed that the film was so

much about family, because I think the families of firefighters are as much the heroes as the men and women in the field fighting fires. They experience virtually everything the firefighters do, both the glory and the tragedy. And I think what *Ladder 49* shows is that it takes a lot of very special, very strong people to allow these guys to do what they do. The irony is that Jack Morrison needs his family to sustain his courage as a firefighter, but his life as firefighter in turn puts his family at risk of losing their father.'

He would spend six weeks at the Baltimore Fire Academy, saying, 'I wanted to personally experience as much as I could about what real firefighters go through. Not just fighting fires but also hitting the books and taking the tests and learning to deal with the public and all the little details that go into creating a firefighter. After that, I signed up with an actual Baltimore firehouse and spent a month with a truck company there, going out to real fires and rescues. All together, it was an amazing experience.

'I don't think they really can say exactly why. I learned that when you go into a burning building, everything in your body tells you "don't go in there". It's smoky, it's dark, it's totally confusing. But there's some kind of instinct that takes over and overcomes all that. There was a poster in the firehouse that said

"Courage is not the absence of fear, but the realisation that there's something more than fear." I think that's what it's about. Guys like Jack realise that no matter how scared they are, no matter how difficult it may be, there's a chance there's someone trapped inside that fire even more scared than they are. And that moves them to act.'

However, the film's producer would recall, 'Interestingly, when I first met Joaquin, he was so terrified of heights, we had to have a little stepladder that took him halfway up the fire pole. He was dripping in sweat. And yet a few months later he was fearlessly going over the side of a fifteen-story building, supported only by a single thin rope. He became so skilled, he did nearly 100 per cent of his stunts himself. There was absolutely no trickery involved.'

The firefighters themselves enjoyed watching actors struggle to keep up with the fitness regime. 'It was comical at times and at other times it was flattering to us to see these strong guys struggle with what we do every day,' commented firefighter Mark Yant. 'But I think what happened along the way is they developed a greater appreciation for what we do and we, in turn, learned to really respect these guys for what they were willing to go through to portray us.'

He also added, 'By that time, I couldn't tell Joaquin

from a regular fireman on the street. The guy has just got it. He fell right into the mode and I'm sure if he wanted to do that line of work he'd make out quite well.'

'For me it was just so important to get every aspect of this story right,' explained Phoenix. 'I wanted to be comfortable in real-life situations. But then, after seeing the real thing, my one fear became whether or not the production would be able to re-create realistic fires on the screen. Fire is such an organic, unpredictable thing – how real could the effects be? So what's really gratifying to me is how amazing the effects team on *Ladder 49* was. The fires they created felt like the real thing and allowed all of us to create something very true in our performances.'

While the main actors were advised to get some fire-fighting experience, Phoenix, typically, took it to extremes – with actor Robert Patrick remembering, 'We all just looked at each other and went, "Wow, we've got a long way (to go) to catch up with him." Around the corner strode this beat-up, scruffiest-looking firefighter I've ever seen – and it was Joaquin.'

After Joaquin's stint had ended, the Baltimore Fire Department said that he could come and get a job any day.

Another actor, Baltimore Getty, recalls, 'We went out on a real call and into a real fire, and there was no supervision. It was just us with the firefighters, and they didn't care. It was exhilarating, and it was scary. You're with these guys in your turnout gear, you've got your tank on your back, and you almost feel like you can walk right into it and not get hurt.

'Once the producers realised what we were doing, they put a stop to it. We got a big memo saying, "You are no longer allowed to do ride-alongs with the fire department."'

Russell responded, 'I wanted the actors to have this immersive experience. And the only way to do that was to train them for their own safety so they'd know what to do with the equipment they had and in case something went wrong. As much as the fire was completely controlled throughout, you could only control it so much.'

John Travolta would play Joaquin's character's mentor in the film – 'I saw it as my personal opportunity to give homage to firefighters because they've meant so much to each of us over the years, and especially now. To me this film is about capturing the humanity of firefighters, rather than the myth. The story reveals that they're just like everyone else in the world with one big difference, which is that every day they lay their lives on the line for everyone else.'

The *Grease* star claimed that Joaquin had been a fan

of his since he was nine – telling the press, 'He has a photo of me from *Urban Cowboy*, from when he was nine. It's the only autograph he ever asked for!'

Said Russell, 'We were so excited to have John be a part of this film, but the challenge was to get around the fact that he's such a huge movie star. I told him right away that he was going to have to go into training with the other guys and that it would be tough and there wouldn't be any kind of special treatment – and it turns out that's exactly what he wanted to hear. In the end, it was the perfect casting because Kennedy is really the big dog in the firehouse, the guy everyone else looks up to, and that dynamic just developed naturally between all these young actors and Travolta.'

The older actor said about his character, 'I think Kennedy makes a very interesting human mistake as a leader in that he gets a bit too close to Jack. My character's got to be the toughest guy on the force, make all the hard decisions, but then he bonds to Jack emotionally to the point that he's like family, and that confuses everything. You have a complicated thing going on between them where Kennedy knows Jack is a good firefighter but he worries about him like he's one of his own. I think this happens in part because Kennedy himself doesn't really have a family – he was married once but it failed because of his commitment to such a dangerous job. So Jack's family almost becomes a substitute for the one my character dreamed about but never had.'

Phoenix said it was probably the most extensive research he had ever done for a role. 'It's a really important obligation to be true to these guys' experiences. It was exciting and terrifying when I went to the training academy and did a few weeks there, and joined this class. I wanted just to experience what it is to be a rookie, and to go through the training and feel the anticipation of being sent to a firehouse, and where are you going to go? All the cadets are trying to figure that out, but it's random. Like, they pick you, and it's not even whether you're going to be on the truck or whether you're going to be on the engine. And you should've seen their faces. I got so excited. It was that amazing, just working with the instructors, and really overcoming some fears.'

During filming Travolta said, 'Well, we were always well protected. I was more concerned about the crew in back of me because they were often exposed to the heat with no protection. But I got burned once by grabbing Joaquin. All the metal on his equipment was heated up by the flames, and I forgot. Take one, and I'm out there being my character, and I'm grabbing and I'm pulling him...'

Phoenix added, 'They have a large semi-truck, the back of a semi-truck that's been converted into this maze. And it's only crawling space. You're on your stomach and they blindfold you, and they put full gear on. You go in, and they shield the door. You lift your head in and go down, and it's this way and that way, and you just start crawling, and you put your head down. Suddenly, there's a drop and you have to turn back around, and figure out how to turn backwards. I loved that.'

The film was originally supposed to be shot in Toronto, but Russell was determined to shoot in Baltimore. The city, which can handle three productions simultaneously, was also the setting for HBO drama *The Wire* while *Ladder 49* was being shot there.

'My feeling was, this is an American story, and I didn't want it to be filmed in Toronto and have it take on the role of "general East Coast city",' Russell said. 'I wanted it to be specific because I believe the more specific you make it, the more universal it becomes.'

Russell added, 'Finding the right locale for this story was key, and Baltimore was the right fit because it's a city with so much character. It's very diverse – it has extreme wealth and also poverty, it has skyscrapers but also quiet working-class neighbourhoods. To me, it's like every great American city rolled into one. The other beautiful thing about it is that it sits on a harbour and I loved the idea of a city of water and fire. Water and fire are such big metaphorical icons in this movie.

'Finally, one of the other reasons I wanted to shoot in Baltimore is that it's a city that has struggled. It's a city on the rebound, but it has had its economic difficulties over the years. So there are a lot of abandoned warehouses that we were able to use for the fire sequences and yet there's also a really strong spirit among the people.'

Director of the Maryland film office, Jack Gerbes, said, 'What's important about this film is not only the big economic impact it's having on the city. But it's done a ton for the firefighters here.

'Often firemen go unheralded. But in this case, they are being looked up to by award-winning actors. According to the fire chief, morale at the station has been boosted significantly. Our hope is this movie will do for firefighters what *Top Gun* did for fighter pilots – make them proud of what they do.'

Jacinda Barrett was cast as Phoenix's wife. Joaquin said, 'What a find she is. I didn't know anything about her and she came in with this wit and strength that I think really elevated our scenes together. It was really exciting to discover her character at the same time as Jack was and be surprised by her wisdom and generosity.'

Said Russell, 'I think Jacinda's role may be the most difficult in the film. Her character's conflict is entirely internal. She's not battling fires, but she has her own battles to deal with, and for a young actress to really be able to go beneath what's happening on the surface and somehow show what's going on inside is very rare. From the first time we saw her read, it was clear Jacinda had a different approach to this character. It's very personal, because she's had this life experience that she brought to the part, but she's also a very talented actress. It was exciting for us to see her take this complicated role and make it a real touchstone for audiences to understand the family side of Jack's life.'

To achieve the real-life scenes, special-effects coordinator Larry Fioritto said was one of the toughest assignments of his 30-year career. 'It's a living, breathing thing. Our cast and crew were going to be right in the middle of these fire situations. There was no other way to do it. We had to create fires so that they could be in there, yet keep them safe.'

Russell said, 'I firmly subscribe to the notion that you make a movie in prep. In this case it couldn't be more true. If you're trying to figure it out on the set with all this stuff going on, it would just be a disaster. We'd still be shooting. So we really did our homework.

If the CGI [computer-generated imagery] fire had

looked right, I probably would have considered using it just for the safety factor. But I saw many tests, and it didn't. Fire is just too random and erratic.'

Russell would admit that two explosions 'went off a little bigger than we expected. Nobody got hurt making the movie, I'm happy to say. At the beginning of the movie there's a floor collapse and Joaquin is sucked into the hole that is created by the collapse. If you look closely on the film you'll see a piece of flaming debris fall within a couple of inches of his face and another one fall on his back, catching his jacket on fire. A split second later he had six firefighters on him, putting him out before he knew he was on fire.'

Another incident saw Phoenix engulfed in flames through the hallway. 'It hit him right in the face mask, rolled over his head, and you can see it on the helmet. You can see the smoke pouring off it. Thank goodness he had his face mask on. That was when I stopped letting him get that close to the fires,' Russell said.

Phoenix said, 'After experiencing what I did in the field and going on real calls, anything I did on the set seemed like nothing. The stairs went out from under me and I slid down and had no idea where I was. I was completely lost. I couldn't see anything. I started panicking and then I remembered what I learned. I put out my arms and spun around until I hit somebody.

'Everything in your body is saying "get out". You can't see, you can't hear – all you hear is the sound of fire. You can't feel anything because you've got on all this gear and big gloves. You never overcome the fear but you learn to control it, and trust the equipment.'

It was an exhaustive shoot, and one that was mentally draining for the actor. But he bagged a lead role in every sense. He is the heartbeat of the film – one that revolves all around his character. Critics, however, didn't warm to *Ladder 49*.

Film 2005's Jonathan Ross said, 'I strain my memory – without success – to think of a recent film which is as substantial a waste of time, money and talent as *Ladder 49*. It may be that in the wake of the understandable surge of sympathy and support which followed the heroism of 9/11, a film based on the professional and personal lives of American firefighters seemed a timely artistic decision and a sound commercial one. But this tired, clichéd film fails completely in its efforts to carry off a satisfying combination of grit and warmth.

'Opposite him [Travolta] Joaquin Phoenix is hopelessly miscast, unable to muster the kind of straightforward, "Ordinary Joe" qualities which would make the character work.'

Another review stated, 'As hokey as it was, *Backdraft*, Ron Howard's 1991 tale of fire-fighting brothers, had a B-movie soul that permitted an interplay of jealousies and rivalries against the backdrop of horrific fires and derring-do. *Ladder 49* mutes even a whisper of fear or animosity. Would any Hollywood film tackle a police department, the military or any other such organisation of skilled fighters without a dose of verisimilitude?'

The reaction was something of a disappointment, to say the least, but Phoenix would gain critical plaudits for *Hotel Rwanda* (2004) – director Terry George's compelling dramatisation of the 1994 Rwandan Genocide.

The director stated, 'This was a story that had to be told, a story that would take cinemagoers around the world inside an event that, to all our great shame, we knew nothing about. But more than that, it would allow audiences to join in the love, the loss, the fear and the courage of a man who could have been any of us – if we ever could find that courage.

'I knew if we got this story right and got it made, it would have audiences from Peoria to Pretoria cheering for a real African hero who fought to save lives in a hell we would not dare to invent. It was a very scary challenge for all of us involved with *Hotel Rwanda*, but that same challenge seemed to invigorate everyone who worked on the film, from our great cast and crew to the extras who rose at dawn in Johannesburg's townships of Alexandra and Tembisa to join us in telling this enormous story. I'm proud of everyone who worked on this film.'

The conflict would be one of the bloodiest in Rwanda's history – with around a million people killed in 100 days. Despite the atrocities, the main talking point was how little media attention was given to the events.

'Ten years on, politicians from around the world have made the pilgrimage to Rwanda to ask for forgiveness from the survivors, and once more the same politicians promise "never again",' added George. 'But it's happening yet again in Sudan, or the Congo, or some Godforsaken place where life is worth less than dirt. Places where men and women like Paul and Tatiana shame us all by their decency and bravery.'

Don Cheadle would play Paul Rusesabagina, a hotelier who sheltered Tutsi refugees despite the danger to his life. Playing a cameraman in the film, Joaquin met with many cameramen and journalists in preparation for the role.

'This story is a painful part of Rwanda's history, but nevertheless, a story that has to be told,' he said. 'Unfortunately, many people, including myself, didn't pay attention and were unaware of the true gravity of the situation. I met with three different guys, and it was very insightful. It was difficult hearing their stories and I think it was also very difficult for them to tell the stories, but we learned a lot about their experiences. These cameramen had covered thirty wars, but they said they had never experienced anything like the Rwandan genocide. One gentleman said a number of his friends had breakdowns after Rwanda, and he cried a number of times while telling me about the things he had seen and experienced in Rwanda. Obviously that helped us in really being aware of the full gravity of the situation.

'I don't know how any of them made it. I don't believe any of them came away unscathed. One cameraman said, "The images I saw will never go away." It was a very powerful experience.'

Speaking about Terry George, he said, 'George is a phenomenal writer. He really is able to document characters' lives and elevate the mundane aspect of a character's life. One of Terry's strengths is his ability to bring together so many different factions of the story and somehow mould them all together coherently. It's rare to find a writer who can stick to the truth and the honesty of the characters. He really cares about what he does and writes from his heart.'

George would rave about Phoenix, 'He's one of those

actors who has the capacity to completely disappear inside a role. You're never sure what the performance will be, but it's always going to be hypnotic. We've been so lucky with this cast. Everyone we asked was really willing to do the film. And when they arrived in South Africa, they were all team players and just got down to business.'

It was in the next few years that Phoenix's true desire for a role came to the fore, a watershed era in his career during which he learnt how to disappear completely.

CHAPTER NINE

PHOENIX CASHES IN

Call it fate or just good-old fashioned luck, but before Phoenix would go on to sign on for the role of a lifetime, he had already met Johnny Cash just months before.

James Gray was shooting some of footage of Cash and June in the studio. Phoenix's name came up and, because Cash was a fan of *Gladiator*, an invite was issued to Joaquin to have dinner with Cash.

Not surprisingly, Phoenix was reluctant. To him, dinner parties where he didn't really know the host and where there were four different knives and forks beside a plate, simply didn't suit him. He thought the request was, well, odd.

Phoenix said, 'I went to have dinner at their house before I even heard about the movie. We were in the living room and John just started strumming. He said he was waiting for June before he could get his nerve up. And I thought, "Wow, this is Johnny Cash waiting to get his nerve up. This guy has played prisons and he's nervous." Then June came in and they started singing "On the Banks of the River Jordan" and they're looking into each other's eyes, and the connection and love they had was palpable.'

He would call the meeting 'ironic and fortunate'.

'Had I not met him, I wouldn't have had that experience and it's pretty extraordinary to me that whether it's by chance or divinity – I don't know what it is that I got to meet him and experience that. To see them looking into each other's eyes while they sang the song was magical. It was just absolutely magical. I referred to that moment many times throughout shooting.'

Gray said to *Huffington Post*, 'We went six years before working together again, though we did see each other frequently in that time and became good friends. We recognised quickly that we had the same tastes; every now and then, we would call each other, usually late at night – did you see that film? What a piece of shit! – and the call would last for hours. I learned, too, that he had admirers from all walks of life. When

Johnny Cash told me he could quote "that Phoenix fella" at will, I decided to put the two of them together for a dinner. What followed was of course a meal for the ages.'

The film came about when James Mangold and his producer Cathy Konrad (who he would later marry) began talking about the idea of a Johnny Cash biopic while on the set of *Cop Land*.

'I remember vividly the excitement Jim [Mangold] and I had when our very first meeting with John and June was set up,' said Konrad. 'We flew down to Hendersonville, Tennessee and they invited us over for breakfast. We were waiting in the lobby of a Holiday Inn and suddenly I heard this booming voice. I turned around to hear: "Hi, I'm Johnny Cash." And there he was, in his boots and jeans. He picked us up in his diesel Mercedes and we went to their house for breakfast. It was a very powerful experience. They said a beautiful grace before breakfast and they sang a song together. It was a day that Jim and I hold very dear.

'As we got to know John better, Jim never shied away from asking him provocative questions that many people might have been afraid to ask. And John really trusted him. Jim inspired a real confidence in John in how Jim was going to tell this story.'

Added Mangold, 'The more I learned from John

about the early years in his life and career, the more I saw an opportunity to make a movie about a time when making music was about making music, and not about money or videos. John's story isn't the tale of some prodigy or raw ambition; he started late, taught himself to play guitar, and got little encouragement. Nobody was beating a path to his door when he moved to Memphis. But John was smart enough to plant himself at Sun [Records], ground zero of a musical revolution. Surrounded by outrageous talent, John grew into something none of the others there would ever be – a timeless storyteller and a searing voice of the shadows. His songs were so unique, so personal, and so raw.

'Of course, the other opportunity was to make a movie about one of the great love stories. There was something magical about the idea that for a decade, the only place John and June were allowed to be alone together was onstage in front of 10,000 people.'

Cash told MTV, 'I had definitely lost my way. 1967 ... I was on amphetamines really, really bad, and I was totally insane. I got in my Jeep and I drove down to Chattanooga, and there was a cave there...a monstrous cave, it went for miles back up onto Lookout Mountain. I went into that cave with my pills, just exploring, you know.

'I had all these wild ideas about finding gold, Civil War [memorabilia] or something in this cave. I'd keep going and I kept taking the pills, kept taking the amphetamines, and after a certain point, after I'd been in there about three hours…I tried to close my eyes, but you can't close your eyes for long on amphetamines. I laid down and I said, "God, I can't take it anymore; I can't make it any further, you'll have to take me now, I want to go, I want to die."

'June … she was my solid rock. She was always there; she was my counsellor, comforter, everything else. What a wonderful woman she was.'

Mangold added, 'Certainly in the time I was talking to John after June's death, for the few months he was alive after that was a very lonely time for him, because he had lost his great companion.'

'We were together forty years,' Johnny Cash said of June. 'We worked on the road together since 1963, and we got married in 1968.' Then, smiling through the pain, he offered up one final pearl of wisdom. 'And the secret for a happy marriage? Separate bathrooms.'

'This is a story very few people know,' said Mangold. 'Young John and his peers were pioneers struggling to find their way. What does it mean to be a rock star when no one has lived that life before you? What do you do with all this attention? How do you handle the pressure, the money, the fans, the demands? There were no roadies, tour buses, five-star hotels, air conditioning or cell phones to stay connected to your family. People like John, Elvis and Jerry Lee were just driving their gear every night from one sweltering gig to another. No one knows how hard these tours were. I thought it was a world I hadn't seen on screen before.'

To play the music legend, Mangold would turn to Phoenix.

'There was just something in Joaquin's eyes. He just had that same sense of searching for something. Joaquin has the honesty that is so much a part of who John was.'

Cash was delighted that Phoenix was playing him, with Mangold remembering, 'He was thrilled, John was a very trusting man. He was very easy-going, a very cool guy. When you've got someone like Joaquin who, frankly, is very similar, a very cool actor, John knew that we were moving in the right direction.'

Phoenix in return was desperate to be in the movie. 'When I heard that James Mangold was directing a movie about the life of Johnny Cash, I wanted to do it without even reading the script. I just had a really good feeling about it, and I liked the idea of playing such a complex man who led an incredibly rich life. Many people only know Johnny Cash as the "Man in Black".

It was exciting for me to learn about his early years and his breakthrough at Sun Records, just as rock and roll was taking off.'

Playing June Carter would be Reese Witherspoon.

'I knew more about the Carter family, actually, than I did about Johnny Cash as a child. We had to study the history of country music in the fourth grade, and that's who we learned about. We did a whole play about the history of country music.

'I just got a call from my agent, and he said that Jim Mangold wanted to meet with me for this script about Johnny Cash. I was immediately interested – even though I didn't know about John, I knew that it was going to be very challenging as an actor. I just had that sense.'

Talking about preparations, including spending months watching him onstage, Phoenix revealed, 'Rather than trying to mimic what John did, I really tried to understand why he did what he did. I saw that John used to lift his head with his chin leading up in the air. I thought it was just kind of a little move that he did, but I realised after a while that he was actually taking a breath of air. So I just naturally started lifting my head to breathe.'

He continued, 'Oh man, there were so many things. I mean, the toughest thing about researching someone like John is that every time you turn the page in his book you go, "Oh, this is amazing. Now how do we not tell this story?" It's really hard but at some point you really have to focus on the story that the director is trying to tell, and look for the research material that includes that.'

He said, 'I spent months rehearsing the singing part and every once in a while I'd think, "I can't sing this! Why don't I just lip-synch it?" I'd call up Reese and tell her I'd quit the singing bit if she did.

'We'd agree to lip-synch for about five seconds – and then revert back to the singing.'

Talking about the decision to sign in the movie, Phoenix said, 'Well, I think from the beginning that was Jim Mangold's hope for whoever played the parts. It's in the spirit of John and June; there's such authenticity and simplicity to their music, so I think that it just seemed the right way to approach it. But neither of us had any experience, so when Jim first brought it up I couldn't say, "Oh yeah, we'll do it" and "That's no problem!"

'But like so many things as an actor that you come against, you always come against experiences that you don't share with the character, and I was up for the challenge. But I didn't want...if the only value of us singing was, "That's Joaquin and Reese really singing",

238

that wasn't enough. It couldn't be a distraction. I didn't want the power to be that we were singing ourselves and that would be the story. We had to get to the place where we were actually telling their story.'

Mangold would turn to award winning roots-rock producer T Bone Burnett to executive-produce the film. He had worked on the *O Brother Where Are Thou?* and they would both devise musical boot camps for Joaquin and Reese. These comprised music lessons, individual practice time, band practice, and practice recording sessions.

Said Burnett, 'Johnny Cash has been so important to me all my life. He's up there with Mark Twain and Walt Whitman as a towering American cultural figure – but at the same time he was also wild and part of the rock-and-roll culture'.

'In a sense, this is the punk Johnny Cash,' he added. 'What set him apart was that he was always going off on his own, doing something unlike anyone else. He was just a completely unique character.'

Witherspoon would note about her singing partner, 'It took us about three months to trust each other because we didn't know each other at all in the beginning and we couldn't even look at each other when we had to sing to each other because it was so embarrassing. I'd sing too loud and he'd say, "It's driving me crazy, she's singing too loud. Does she have to sing so loud?" I said, "I'm just trying here!"

'It took about three months before we responded to each other's work and saw improvement. It took a long time before we really felt comfortable with each other.'

Once that happened, she added, 'There were days we felt bad. He would say, "You're doing really good today," or, on days he felt like crap, I said, "Don't beat yourself up, you're doing a really good job." We really leaned on each other and became close in that way.

'It's helpful to go through that process with someone; you don't feel so frightened and alone. He was very committed to the role, and he practiced really hard, and worked that guitar.'

Talking about learning the guitar, he said, 'It's amazing to create something out of nothing. It's a piece of a fucking tree! And it's completely foreign to me; you don't even know how to hold the thing and what to do. Then to play a C chord and to hear something in your head and go, "Ah, it's a G! So C foes into G! It's wild, because it seems endless, the possibilities for discovery, and yet you are very very limited, because there only so many chords in Western music, and so many notes.

'One thing that was important to me was how Johnny had gone through an evolution. He wasn't born the Man in Black. That stage persona and that voice that became so recognisable were not what he started with. When I heard these early recordings of him I was really surprised. There were some songs where I listened with T Bone and I asked, "Are you sure this is Johnny Cash?" I started looking at a lot of artists and their evolution, especially those with a strong persona like David Bowie, John Lennon. Very rarely does it come along and, at the peak of their careers, they are as they started, it is always an evolutionary process. I thought I would rather see that in a film.'

Sight & Sound's review would state, 'From the crackly incompetence of his fumbling audition for Sam Phillips with "two mechanics who can't hardly play", to the growling menace of his "man in black" persona from whose rumbling larynx issued forth the voice of death, Phoenix manages the exact stance (hoiked shoulders), gait (uncertain, yet unstoppable) and sheer derailed presence of a man who lived his life as if on his way to a funeral ("maybe I am", Johnny repeatedly opines).'

Reese Witherspoon said the live performances in the movie were the hardest thing she'd ever done. 'You can't imagine how nerve-wracking it is to be on stage in front of an audience and have to sing when you've never professionally done so. But it was also a lot of fun learning to adapt and dive into something so completely outside the comfort zone.'

Mangold said, 'Neither John nor June would sit around bragging about their vocal dexterity. They've done brilliant vocal work but you don't necessarily want a trained singer to play them. I always felt that what you need to play them is most of all authenticity, and Joaquin and Reese were committed to that.'

One of the more obvious questions that Joaquin would face in interviews would of course involve similarity between him and Cash in that both had lost brothers. Phoenix would say, 'I think people have an idea of what my experience is and they think that's what it is. But it's not. My experience is very different from John's. I think there's a vast difference with your understanding of life and death when you're ten years old to when you're eighteen.

I've never found it beneficial to draw from my personal life, I don't think it honours John's experience and I don't think it honours Jack's experience by imposing my idea of things upon them. I simply filled everything in his life story and broke it down in segments – John and June, John and his music, John and Jack, and I never once had to imagine, "How does John feel in this situation?" I had all these other sources of information and always drew from that.'

He would, however, get angry over reports that a scene involved him recalling the death of his older brother in the film. It was rumoured that he kept banging his head on the bedpost, and had to be taken away in an ambulance.

Phoenix ranted in response to the *New York Daily News*, 'That's not the way my brain works. You know, the press has kind of imposed upon me the title of Mourning Brother, and because I haven't been vocal about it, the assumption is that I'm holding on to it and all this shit that's just not there. I don't need to pull from my experience for a character, and I've never understood why actors would, except for lack of ability, imagination or research.

'I had all three things, so this is a little frustrating to me, because it denies my work and the research that I did.'

He was still struggling with TV interviews. He was scheduled to appear on *The Oprah Winfrey Show* – a US national institution that understandably terrified the actor. In fact he was so nervous Oprah had to come into the green room to coax him into doing the interview. Not the usual way for actors to behave – they normally couldn't wait to come out and talk about themselves.

She said, 'Nervous is not the word. He was a wreck.

I've never seen nervous like that before. I had to go in the green room, and literally say to him, "You don't have to put yourself through this." He said, "I think I'm going to throw up."'

The film *Walk The Line* was released in 2005 and would go on to be a hit both critically and commercially, with *The Hollywood Reporter* saying, 'Phoenix has never been the most expressive of actors, but that works just fine for Johnny Cash. A shy man who cultivated an outlaw image and sang of hard-luck lives in hard-living songs, he took the stage with a stony face and a guitar aimed at the audience. Phoenix doesn't look much like Johnny, but he gets his stage persona.'

When he was Oscar nominated for the role, Joaquin said, 'I mean, I don't really like the idea of competition, and it's such a subjective thing, what's good, and I hate the whole idea of one person being the best anything, in a sense. But what it translates to, for me, is that people are responding to this film in an emotional way, and for a movie that almost didn't get made and was nine years in the making from when Jim Mangold first optioned the rights, it's a wonderful thing and it's affecting people.'

But he would once again lose out.

Reese Witherspoon did, however, win the Academy Award for best actress.

It would be another film that he refused to watch

himself in. 'I just don't find it beneficial as an actor. There's a danger in watching oneself. I think it breeds a certain self-awareness that isn't helpful. There are actors that I admire, but I've noticed that throughout their career they just seem to be repeating themselves and making the same faces almost. I theorise, and I don't know, but I think it's from watching oneself over and over and seeing that "Oh, audiences seem to respond when I do this" or "I look best when I do this" or "I look worst when I do this" and I don't think that that's helpful, so I just don't watch them.'

Snyder commented, 'It's common for actors not to watch themselves. Usually they get annoyed or resentful because they feel that they gave a better performance on the day than is on the screen and can't understand why the director never used that take.'

Phoenix would say about his experience of making the film, 'The hardest thing in some ways is to remain stimulated by a role throughout the course of a three-month shoot and twice as long to prep. I never had that problem with John. He was an incredibly complex person, and there are so many beats to play that I never once felt bored by him. I always felt challenged.'

He was to find the role hard to shake off – blaming the personal troubles that followed on his inability to return to normal once it wrapped.

'Every movie soaks into you for a certain amount of time. It's like growing a beard: tiny steps, little growth. Suddenly your beard is whacked off and you say, "Fuck me! I'm naked!" You can no longer rely on the world that you have created. The rug has been pulled from under you and suddenly there's...nothing. The job finishes and you say, "What do I do? How do I act? What is my life?" It can be very lonely,' Phoenix said.

'I went through confusion and depression. After a film like this, I lose those things that help define me and make me comfortable. I go through this thing of, "What am I? What do I do?"' Joaquin added. 'I know all this sounds so fucking serious, but I don't know why I like acting so much or why I like getting into a role. I don't want anything else that comes with acting, like the fame or the so-called perks.'

He went on to say how much he threw himself into a role, that he abandoned his life when he worked. 'I don't wear the clothes or listen to the music that defines who I am. I don't communicate with friends or family. It sounds intense, but it's the process of getting there that is really hard.

'It's always been the case for me. If I play a waiter I'll get a job as a waiter. Expectations are low because we're accustomed to shortcuts in acting, but I think we have a sense of when something is authentic and when it isn't. With this part I didn't think I had to sound like Cash, but I certainly had to know how he felt when he was singing.'

In another interview he was quoted as saying, 'I felt abandoned when it [the film] was over, totally cut loose without a lifeline. This was the longest I'd ever worked on something. All I did every day was read about John or listen to John. Everything was John.'

He admitted himself to rehab.

Talking about his experience, he said, 'To be honest I don't know how comfortable I am saying that I'm an alcoholic. Not because I think it's shameful, but I just don't know if it's true. I prefer sobriety. In the past, if I had to go to an event where there was a lot of small talk, I'd think, "I can't handle this". So I would just drink and not care. That was the extent of my alcoholism. When I'm working, I get very motivated, but there's part of me that loves the idea of doing nothing, and drink allows you to do nothing. Now I'm forced to do something more worthwhile with my friends. I used to think people were pussies to not drink. Now I think it's courageous.'

On his experience of rehab he said, 'It was really more of a country club that didn't serve booze. You fall into routines. But I didn't want to go out and feel I have to fucking drink just to be okay with going to a restaurant.

Yet the temptation was too great. But I honestly don't know what I think of myself as an alcoholic. I don't sit there yearning for a drink.'

Another incident saw him famously stop mid-sentence during press interviews to state to a stunned room, 'Do I have a large frog in my hair?'

Journalist: 'No, no'.

Phoenix: 'Something's crawling out of my scalp.'

Journalist: 'No, you look great.'

Phoenix: 'No, but I feel it. I'm not worried about the looks. I'm worried about the sensation of my brain being eaten... What did you ask me?'

His publicist said afterwards, 'I think a fly flew on his head. I was standing right there and was laughing with him. He then went right back to the press line. He's doing interviews every damn day And, no, he's not having a nervous breakdown and is still sober. He's fantastic.'

Several months after rehab, Phoenix was driving a car down a winding road in Hollywood, when his car flipped over. Bloodied, bruised and shaken, he was about to light a cigarette when a man called out. 'Just relax.' Phoenix replied, 'I'm fine. I am relaxed.' The man replied, 'No, you're not' – pointing out that he was about to light a cigarette in a car that was leaking petrol.

The man turned out to be eccentric German director Werner Herzog.

Phoenix said, 'I remember this knocking on the passenger window. There was this German voice saying, "Just relax." There's the air bag, I can't see and I'm saying, "I'm fine. I am relaxed."

'Finally, I rolled down the window and this head pops inside. And he said, "No, you're not." And suddenly I said to myself, "That's Werner Herzog!" There's something so calming and beautiful about Werner Herzog's voice. I felt completely fine and safe. I climbed out.'

'I got out of the car and I said, "Thank you". And he was gone.'

Herzog would recall the encounter two years later, 'Nothing mysterious, there was a car in front of me on a steep hill in Hollywood Hills and I saw it was too fast and not under control; it was apparently a failure of brakes and I knew it was not going to end well, the car overturned and it came to a rest on its roof and it was pretty much smashed in. Since I was in the car right behind it, I jumped out and tried to quickly assess how many people were in there and what could I do. I saw one man and it was Joaquin.

'Now comes the moment where I see him apparently unhurt, I mean he was in shock, apparently physically unhurt and I see him fumbling with a cigarette and cigarette lighter, but on the other side the car's gasoline is

249

dripping. I asked for the cigarette lighter. And then other people came and we got him out. I knew he wanted to thank me and shake my hands, but I didn't want to make a fuss and I drove off. That was my encounter.'

His publicist said the next morning, 'His brakes went out and the car flipped over. But he's doing fine. He may be very sore in the morning, but right now he is doing okay.'

There were understandably worries that Joaquin was dealing with fame the same way his late brother had. His press conferences were becoming more erratic – as were his interviews.

One such interview had him quoted as saying, 'The one question I've been getting is: "Do you take this home with you?" And the truth is, no. But people don't want to hear that. So it's a weird situation, because you either tell people the truth, which is that there isn't a whole lot going on, and then they don't think highly of you. Or you just lie, which I do a million times. "Oh yes, it's really hard to sleep at night." Yeah, it's real hard to sleep when you have production assistants who will get you anything you want. You're on a set where people are constantly taking care of you. It's a piece of cake.

'I never prepare. I think that's completely overrated. It's a very simple job. All you have to do is hit this bright mark, stand in the right spot and say the line. So I don't really believe in preparation.'

When reminded of all the training he did for *Ladder 49*, he said, 'I just said that because I thought it would sound good to the press. Look, there are preparation changes every time. I don't know why it seems to be of note that actors do any kind of preparation. It's just what you're supposed to do in your fucking job. Do you think that because you did some research that you deserve some special credit?'

An insider on the movie told this writer, however, 'He did about a month-and-a-half's worth of research and preparation. It was extensive, enrolling in the actual Baltimore fire academy and living at a fire house itself. It should also be noted that the other actors followed his lead and did the same. Research and preparation are crucial for him as an actor, so I can only presume he was being glib with the interviewer.'

Even so, the seeds were sown in people's minds – perfect if you wanted to play a self-destructive prank a few years down the line.

CHAPTER TEN
HELLO, GOODBYE

Next would be gritty drama *Reservation Road* that, while praised for its gritty drama, would fail to find an audience. Reuniting with Terry George, it told the story of two fathers involved in a tragic accident that would destroy both their lives.

Phoenix claimed, 'I had a visceral reaction to the script. I liked that it was a thriller, but most interesting to me was it successfully telling two sides of the same story: both Ethan and Mark are fully realised, completely different and unique. Terry George understands deep emotions, yet he is unsentimental; I knew he would find the right balance. On the set and during takes, we would make discoveries in the moment, which I already knew Terry to be very good at.'

He went on to explain how the journey of making a movie was mysterious at the start. 'You don't really know what you are going to end up with, which is part of the joy and excitement of making a film. Why *Reservation Road* was one of the hardest I've done, and I think maybe why Jennifer [Connelly] felt it was *the* most difficult one she's done, was because each scene was a discovery. Having not rehearsed, we went in never really knowing the answer. We had freedom in terms of movement because Terry used multiple cameras, a lot of which were hand-held.'

Mark Ruffalo, who also starred, and Phoenix loved working together – with the former labelling Joaquin as the new Brando. Phoenix was quick to return the compliment.

'I remember when I saw *You Can Count on Me* I nearly retired. I thought, "Whoever this Mark Ruffalo is, he's the best and he's doing something really special." He's just an incredible actor. It was very fortunate for us that Mark wanted to be part of this journey. As a fellow actor, he turned out to be constantly surprising and emotionally available, with a brilliant understanding of character and story.'

Ruffalo added, 'The initial plan was that Joaquin

and I would never see each other until it came time to do our scenes together. But we hit it off pretty strongly, so we ended up hanging out a lot. He's one of our best actors, and I knew I could learn quite a bit from him working on the film – which I did. He is generous and thoughtful.'

'There's a truthfulness about Joaquin that keeps you grounded,' Terry George said. 'He will not let something stay in, or play out, if he thinks it's false or doesn't ring true. For a director, that's an emotional lifeline.'

Incidentally, Ruffalo was originally supposed to play Joaquin's part in *Signs* but had to pull out, and Phoenix was linked to the role of the The Hulk in the upcoming *Avengers* movie – before losing out to Ruffalo.

It would be something of a *The Yards* reunion in *We Own The Night* (2007) – with Joaquin again teaming up with James Gray and Mark Wahlberg. Gray actually wrote the parts with the two actors in mind. Producer Nick Wechsler said, 'James developed such a strong rapport with these two actors. He was thinking of them throughout his research and writing process – it was almost like a shortcut to making a successful movie.'

Gray said in the press notes, 'This is a film that works in a specific and familiar genre – the police movie. But normally the police movie focuses on procedure finding the bad guy. I wanted to do something much more focused on character and emotion. The genre becomes a point of departure to tell a story about a man caught by his destiny, his inevitable fate, and the complex and internally conflicted emotions that love, loss and betrayal yield.'

The film would feature Wahlberg and Phoenix playing two brothers on different sides of the law. Their father was played by Robert Duvall, who was amused at the intensity Phoenix displayed on set, saying, 'He was always invading my space on camera. I think it was a device they had to get me a little irritated. It kinda worked in a way.

'I was glad I could play it – and work with these very talented people. Joaquin, or Wackeen as I call him, and Mark are really talented guys.'

While Wahlberg would be in awe working with *The Godfather* star, Gray noticed, 'Duvall can't stand that respect or distance. He likes to feel like he's in the trenches with them. But Joaquin would do everything he could do to really get Duvall's character angry with him. He even wore an earring strictly so that Duvall would look at him and think "you little wimp".'

'On the other side,' Gray continued, 'Mark Wahlberg was telling me, "Don't bother Duvall, Jim. He's a great actor." And their dynamic mirrored the respectful dynamic of Burt and Joseph in the film.'

The idea all started when Gray was asked to write a movie about cops that had a car chase. 'I was anxious to make something not just thrilling, but explosive, dramatic. And frankly, filled with action – of course, there's that car chase. This is a very personal movie; that doesn't mean autobiographical. As I was writing the screenplay, I used elements that came from local news stories as well as things I learned by going on police ride-alongs. I found many stories about people who, because of their circumstances, hid their family connections to the police. Everything you see in the film came from real events, but I also used my relationships with my father and brother. So I did steal a lot from my background as well.'

Said Phoenix: 'James cares. He truly cares about film. In an age of such self-conscious irony, that is a rare quality. James is willing to dig through glass to uncover the truth in each moment, and he stimulates those around him to do the same. I couldn't wait to get back into the ring with him and explore the emotional machinations of this family.'

Wahlberg added, 'James is incredibly talented and working with him and Joaquin on *The Yards* was a great experience. I was especially flattered that he wrote the part of Joseph in *We Own the Night* for me.'

Gray added, 'Joaquin calls Duvall the Jedi master. You can throw Duvall any curve ball and he'll come right back at you in character and he'll do something amazing. The level of the craft is ridiculous.'

Reviews on the film were generally mixed, with the *LA Times* stating, 'Though it's not quite film noir, *We Own the Night* has a darkly brooding style that suits the material. Screenwriter/director James Gray (*The Yards*) does a better job directing than writing. Some of the story becomes melodramatic, and the dialogue can be banal, but the performances are strong, marked by conflicted emotions. There are some well-played lines, such as "Better to be judged by 12 than carried by 6," along with such prosaic exhortations as, "You're going to get yourself killed!"

'The movie really belongs to Phoenix, who gives a haunting performance with just the right degree of intensity. Though the story – a cops-vs-gangsters contest with undercurrents of a Cain-and-Abel saga – is not breaking any new ground, it has a resounding redemptive quality that draws us in.'

Roger Ebert noted, 'But this is an atmospheric, intense film, well acted, and when it's working it has a real urgency. Scenes where a protagonist is close to being unmasked almost always work.'

Phoenix would work with Gray again on *Two Lovers* (2008) – which focuses on a young man who moves back to his parents' house following a suicide attempt. He then meets two women – Vinessa Shaw and Gwyneth Paltrow – one a sweet girl who is the daughter of his father's business partner; the other a beautiful but unpredictable neighbour.

'Joaquin feels like a brother to me and that's a very rare thing,' said Gray. 'I'm very close with him. We talk about what it is we want to explore in people. Joaquin has an unbelievable eye for human behaviour and a really great understanding of what people are about and what motivates them. Frankly he likes the same things that I like, so of course I would always want to work with him.

'Joaquin is a brilliant actor but he's also an unbelievably hard worker and people don't understand that about him. What he's always asking is "What can I bring to it?" "What detail can I bring to it that makes it sing with life?" So I always try to look for that extra touch that makes his performance unique. Joaquin focuses on his own character and is very single-minded about it. He doesn't see his own movies because for him it's all about the process. In that sense he's a true artist because he doesn't care about what other people think about his performance or his character, whether he is liked or hated and that's also incredibly rare.'

Gray did admit however that he had concerns about the differences in Joaquin's and Gwyneth Paltrow's acting styles.

'Joaquin likes many takes and a lot of improvisation,' he said. 'He like's it to be very loose and free flowing. Gwyneth likes doing three takes at the most and is extremely precise in that way. Neither technique is better than the other. I love them both, but they're very, very different. And that's a strange mix.'

Paltrow said, 'James is exceptional. He really loves the actor, and you feel very valued and very supported. He laughs hysterically when he likes something you have done, even to the point of ruining takes! At first it was slightly off-putting but then it became very endearing. It's just nice to work with somebody who is so dedicated and who has such a specific vision.

'I laugh when I see things on screen that I like because it feels honest to me and I didn't expect it. Human behaviour is very funny, it's very idiosyncratic and it's very silly. There's a great quote by a director in the Hollywood system, Ernst Lubitsch, and he said, "Even the most dignified person is ridiculous at least twice a day." And that's what movies are; movies are showing the most dignified person during these times because movies are about the extremes of behaviour.'

And of working with Phoenix: 'It has been one of the top two experiences of my life in terms of working with an actor and in terms of being awed by an actor. He's so brilliant, and he's so creative, and inventive. I just feel very impressed by him.'

The film would give Joaquin his best reviews to date. Contactmusic.com wrote about the film: '*Two Lovers* remains, however, an acting exhibition for Phoenix, a far stronger performer than even the competent Paltrow, whose role demands she keep up with him at times. His "acting" is hidden, his raw mumble packed with emotion, much of it unspoken. As Leonard's final motives become clear, Gray lets the viewer in close enough to connect with the character, to sympathise with how decisions can establish a life's path – or alter it in the blink of an eye.'

But it was his behaviour during promotion of the film that Joaquin has become best known for.

At a red carpet event, Phoenix told a reporter, and soon the world, that he was quitting movies and was going to be a rapper.

Gray wrote in *MovieMaker* magazine, 'Joaquin Phoenix announced his retirement recently, and though I was profoundly disappointed, I can't say I was surprised. Joaquin is best described as a mercurial person, so there's a chance he might yet change his mind (selfishly, I hope he does). But his decision is consistent with the person he is and was and always will be.

'Joaquin doesn't care about anything but the work, and even then he cares only about process – never the product (he doesn't even watch his own movies). The young man gave acting everything he had. Perhaps he just ran out of gas. I know now how hard it is to find a true original like him, and that for a time I simply got lucky.'

The director went on to look back at his time with the actor. Talking about *The Yards*, he said, 'I seem to remember a whole lot of torment and angst and yelling and screaming. But I also remember consistently being amazed by the emotional depth of the then twenty-four-year-old. I loved his feral unpredictability; he seemed ready to explode at any minute. He was hard on himself – a true perfectionist – though just as often, his fury was directed at me. I didn't care. We had one thing in common and that was a total commitment to the work.

'At the end of *Two Lovers*, Joaquin seemed simultaneously exhausted and bored. He'd left most of us in the dust long ago. Perhaps that's why he's done with acting: When you can do it all yourself and your genius has outgrown the mediocrity of others, why bother?'

Paltrow said at a press junket, 'I'm not totally convinced this is his last film. There may be something going on. I'm not sure what. It was like a performance, it was brilliant. Maybe it's performance art or something.'

She was of course referring to an upcoming interview with David Letterman. With the media still scrambling around trying to make sense of his retirement, Joaquin was going to be interviewed by US chat show host David Letterman. On 11 February 2009, Joaquin appeared in the *Late Show* studio. Gone were the movie-star good looks – instead, what stood there was a ferociously bearded, heavy-set man, clad in a smart suit and wearing sunglasses. Phoenix mumbled, Letterman goaded and soon everyone feared he was going through a public meltdown.

It was everywhere – skits would appear on TV and the internet; doctors would diagnose Joaquin from that interview alone as being in need of serious medical help. Relationships expert and author of *The Secret Psychology of How We Fall in Love*, Paul Dobransky, floated a theory that Phoenix might be schizophrenic, pointing to his 'socially inappropriate behaviour', including his abrupt career change, poor hygiene and grooming, vocal tics and lack of facial emotion as proof.

'There is something wrong. It's beyond drug abuse,' he said.

Phoenix's publicist, Susan Patricola, branded Dobransky's analysis 'wildly inappropriate'.

'How absolutely inappropriate for a doctor who has no personal interaction or relationship with someone to diagnose them. And to do so in a public forum. Hope they spelled his name right. Another fifteen-minute "expert" is born!'

Everyone asked the same question: 'Was it a hoax?'

Well, yes it was.

And even during the Letterman interview there are two telling signs. One was at the end, when thinking the cameras had stopped, when they were just merely pulling away, you see Joaquin remove his glasses to warmly thank the host. Also, despite the awkward pauses and the reluctance to answer any of Letterman's questions, he is still very composed and sure of himself. But Joaquin Phoenix is terrified of press interviews – especially one where he is coming off as badly as he was. His interview with Jay Leno during *Gladiator* is just as cringeworthy – he's all nervous, fidgety, making inappropriate comments and constantly looking to his family, who are in the audience, for support.

Tickled by how people believed reality shows were real just because it was packaged as such, Casey Affleck and Joaquin wondered if they could do a hoax at a bigger scale. 'I wanted to make a movie with my friends and make one in a different way. I wanted to have a different experience, and I'm really happy to have done that,' Joaquin said. This different 'experience' eventually came to fruition in *I'm Still Here* (2010), one of the most intriguing pieces of performance art ever to be committed to film.

Speaking of the moment when Joaquin was going to announce that he was quitting prior to going on to film an 18-month-long sojourn into hip-hop musicianship, Phoenix leaned over to Casey: '[I asked], "Is this, like, the moment? Shall I announce my retirement right now?" And [Casey] said, "Yes". It wasn't planned.'

Said Joaquin, 'At some point, [my reinvention] became such a public spectacle. To be frank, we were kind of hostage to the process. There were times, honestly, where I wanted out. Even on a conventional film, I'm done after four months. But this went on and on.'

Affleck told of his attempt to perpetuate the hoax: 'It was challenging. It was probably one of the better film-making experiences I've ever had. I learned an enormous amount. I sort of did the whole thing by myself because I started really small, and I thought, "Won't this be an interesting experiment?" I don't think anyone else has the opportunity to make this kind of a movie.

'I don't remember this movie being made, really – unless it's like *Don't Look Back*. But in *Don't Look Back*, there was still a distance between the filmmaker and the subject. They didn't have video, for one thing. There were certain advantages that I had. I could shoot 450 hours of somebody just picking their toes. It just so happened that it was two years of just the opposite.

'There was a small amount of toe-picking, but there was a lot of really, really dramatic, interesting stuff that happened in his life over the course of those two years, and he let me capture it. In that way, I feel like I just lucked out.'

It was an idea that Joaquin and Casey had had in their heads for a while, and one, understandably, where they would constantly begin to feel insecure about. Before the David Letterman interview, it would have been easy to call time on the project. Shooting on the film was stop, start, stop, start. They would work on it, then Joaquin would have second thoughts and quit, before going back to work on it once more.

Once his 'breakdown' became public, he had no choice but to persevere. Not that he would still have huge doubts, needing Casey to plead with him to keep going. The idea stemmed from Joaquin being a self-obsessed actor frustrated at his success, and deciding to prove his talents elsewhere. Set against a backdrop of the media's glare fully on him sealed the deal for Casey.

The Letterman interview was, to use an American expression, a home run – a banker, thanks to Joaquin's 'Was-he, wasn't-he faking' deadpan performance and David Letterman's goading. If Letterman wasn't in on the act, and that look at Joaquin's almost apology to Letterman as the camera pulls away (Casey was furious that Joaquin slipped out of character for a brief second), would give fire to that argument. They couldn't have asked for a more perfect host: he was so vicious, relentless in his goading of the easy target this bearded, overweight talent presented to him, that it bordered on cruelty.

Another opportunity that was presented to them was the heckler rapper moment. To the crowd's chagrin, Joaquin appeared on stage four hours later than billed for a performance, and duly launched an expletive-filled attack on one of the audience members after they 'voiced' their dissatisfaction. Joaquin was always going to goad the heckler with his pay cheque, but what they weren't expecting was that the crowd would cheer the actor, wanting him to dish out more verbals to the heckler.

Joaquin and Affleck's plan to create a sort of homage to *Seinfeld* star Michael Richard's racial outburst, where the audience had turned on him, backfired. To Joaquin's utter bemusement the crowd 'fucking cheered'. But in the end it played out perfectly. Joaquin used the audience's cheers not to play up to adulation but to fuel his disgust at them and himself – throwing himself into the crowd.

Despite a staff member at Letterman claiming it was staged, the US TV personality still maintains that he had no idea. However, Joaquin said in a 2000 interview that he was stunned to find out that the banter is prepared beforehand by an underling. He preferred Letterman because 'We have an unspoken agreement that I'm going to fuck off, he plays straight and I play crazy.'

While the nature of the film would ebb and flow, it was meticulously planned. They had no idea how the public would bend this story they presented to the world, but they made sure they had every base covered. The crux of the story sees Joaquin retiring movies to become a rapper. To recruit Sean Combs, the pair headed out to Miami. Heralded a 'genius' by Joaquin, he was delighted that Combs was game for their ideas straight away. Sensing his enthusiasm, Affleck shot one of their scenes together that night. For about an hour, they managed three takes – resulting in one of the highlights of the film, and one that was used as a teaser.

It was improvisation, and as such some days went smoother than others. When Joaquin was tired, it was left to Affleck to raise his spirits and, at times, use some other techniques. For a director to constantly judge the energy of a room and manipulate that constantly can be a draining experience – even more so when it's done with a group of friends, who would be chatting away one minute and then having to dive into an intense scene the next.

For one of the scenes where Joaquin gets angry with Anthony Langdon, Affleck could see that his star wasn't up for it. He was exhausted. But for Affleck, it was their last night in New York, and the scene had to happen. As Joaquin remember it, Affleck barged into Ant's room and started shouting at him, 'Why aren't you putting the tapes together, where are the lights?'

Joaquin recalled to *Flaunt* magazine, 'And so I walked into the room and was like, "Where are the fucking lights? Why are you always fucking everything up?" And that's what happened a lot. A lot of the energy in the room Casey would have to create and star and let it warm, and then I would come in.'

The much-talked-about scene – and certainly the one

269

that had everyone talking during industry screenings –
was the 'Grand Dumping' scene.

Casey and Joaquin had always planned something
traumatic to happen to him, and they talking about
several options. But it was Joaquin who was obsessed
with having a 'friend' defecate on his face. Both were in
no doubt that it was a cheap and easy joke, but were
both canny enough, or cynical, depending on your
point of view, to realise that it would be one that would
be most talked about.

His friends were amazed at his appearance, at how
much weight he had put on and the disregard he
showed for his appearance. However, Casey wryly
noted that it was more than just the simple act of
putting on weight to get into character. There was
method to the madness – in which Joaquin would still
resemble someone with some sort of control over
himself despite the apparent disregard of vanity. He
would make sure he got a nice suit and would wear it
most times he went out in public, to ensure that he had
some semblance of looking good.

The plan had actually been for him to be in better
shape than normal, the idea being that he would be super
vain and muscled up. However, Affleck felt that an actor
imploding would be better suited to the appearance that
Joaquin would later adopt.

Affleck would add to *Flaunt* magazine, 'Some of the people on the film were chosen not for the roles they had on the crew, but because they were going to play characters in the movie as well – they would be part of the cast. This is a movie about a man having a movie made about him. He alienates everyone until the only people around make up a documentary film crew. Then he alienates the film crew. So some of the crew were chosen as much as for their real personality and how well suited they would be as a "cast member" as they were for what they could do on the crew.'

Trust was essential between Joaquin and Casey, and the actor gave his director all of his. He would perform scenes willingly, and with total trust in his director. He had no idea the scenes he shot with the prostitutes, which was shot over two nights, would segue into one.

Affleck added, 'Well, there were some who did think that what was happening was real, even people on the crew. And that did two things, really. It made for some really great reactions and a genuinely tense environment on the set that we needed. It created confusion for some people. Real emotions came into play. Nobody was hurt and everyone was told what was happening, but, honestly, Joaquin was so believable at times and so committed and so relentlessly in character that people got confused. And it was my job to help create, sustain or squash that confusion when the scene we were shooting demanded it. And that created more confusion. But that too was a performance because the film is in part about a man and his relationship to the people making a film about him.'

Fifteen years before, Affleck would call the tabloids and tell them where they were and would stage a fight. Problem is, that fifteen years ago, no one cared and the handful of fake fights fell on deaf ears.

Joaquin told the press, 'Casey was going around doing press for a movie, and he wanted to wear a beard for the interviews, and they wouldn't allow him to. And I saw a picture of me recently with a beard, and I was like, wow, that was the beard that Casey was trying to do, fifteen years ago, and he finally got it in there. Looking back, over the course of knowing each other for twenty years, all the things we've talked about, all the things we've wanted to do, and we always wanted to do a movie with each other and with our friends. That there was a way to do it – you didn't need to do it with 150 people and make-up and hair.

'And we had Larry, who's a production designer, and does special effects and props, and has worked on movies and done all of those things, so we know that he could do those things. And he had great ideas for the house, and building up the studio, and putting the posters up, and so we just felt that we had and knew the friends to make it in a way that we wanted to make it, so it's actually been a twenty-year process to make this movie.'

Affleck added, 'Joaquin did the concert in Miami. The crowd showed up in fake beards and with cell phone cameras ready to go. They wanted him to make an ass of himself. They wanted to see the Joaquin they saw on Letterman make a fool of himself. When Joaquin jumped off the stage at the heckler, who's a great actor by the way – Eddy Rouse. Really good. He had more in the movie but it had to get cut. So anyway, Joaquin jumped off the stage after one song. His fall from grace was complete. And then they started cheering him on. They chanted his name. The crowd came to life with so much energy. That club was buzzing electric for hours. They were exhilarated, like a high, and then it wore off and they left looking vacant.'

Even the scene at the start, which was apparently home footage of the young Joaquin and his siblings swimming in Panama under the guidance of his father, was in fact shot in Hawaii with actors, and tampered with, in a bid to degrade the images.

While the film isn't real, to put yourself through it

for two years would suggest something self-destructive was deep-rooted in Joaquin's psyche. Perhaps it was the sense of control that the film allowed Joaquin to have, while at the same time allowing him not to care about things that didn't matter to him. There was a heightened sense of paranoia certainly, but knowing that you were being watched must have held a certain appeal. He would parade around the house convinced that Affleck was filming him. On one occasion he delivered a two-hour monologue when there was no camera.

An in-joke among friends is one thing, but it's hard to sustain for two years. There must have been a huge appeal in just saying what you want with the luxury of making it into a documentary.

As Winer has said, Joaquin's greatest gift is his vulnerability. It seemed Joaquin not only sensed this but manipulated it to his own ends. That's *I'm Still Here*'s greatest legacy: an actor fully aware of what he is, and what he can get away with.

The reviews, while kinder in the UK, received a generally hostile reaction from US critics. Roger Ebert called it a 'sad and painful' documentary.

The *New York Daily News* said, 'The whole thing is such a tedious, foul-mouthed mess that it isn't even worth discussing as a riff on the Bob Dylan doc *Don't*

Look Back or a meditation on slovenly semi-madness…
The whole thing is pointless and disgusting.'

The *New York Times* would call it 'a deadpan
satire'. However, *USA Today* spoke for many US
critics, after writing, 'Let's hope that *I'm Still Here* …
is a hoax or some brand of cinematic performance
art. Otherwise, it's an annoying, exploitative and
disturbingly voyeuristic excuse for a film. And whether
truth or folly, it's not particularly well made. Even in
the midst of Phoenix's most oddball and obsessive
torment, it's boring.'

The critic from *Washington Post* simply asked,
'Have we all been punked? Well, maybe. If the whole
movie is an act, it's an Oscar-worthy one.'

The *Guardian* wrote, 'Is this a genuine exercise in
cinéma vérité, cruelly observing the public and private
unwinding of a deeply disturbed man incapable of
handling his career? After all, Phoenix had a troubled
upbringing by a footloose hippy couple, members of a
religious cult, whose five children supported them by
performing in the streets as they drifted around North
and South America. He twice dropped out of acting, just
before and after his [older] brother River Phoenix's
sensational death. Or is *I'm Still Here* a brilliantly
sustained if embarrassing faux-documentary criticising
the cult of celebrity, the media and a gullible public?'

Affleck would attribute the hostile reaction from both critics and cinemagoers to not knowing what was real and what was not. There was a trick being played on them, and they weren't happy about it. When he finally admitted that it was all a performance by Joaquin, he steered clear of the word hoax – merely saying, 'We wanted to create a space. You believe what's happening is real. There were multiple takes, these are performances.'

Affleck told Jay Leno, 'You know, I never did [receive any worried calls].

'Afterward, the movie comes out, the critics liked to say, "This is crazy, this is disturbing, this is sick and we should be worried about him," but while it was happening, people were happy just to mock him.'

He added, 'I wanted them [the audience] to think it was real while they were watching it. But I assumed, when it was over, they would understand that it wasn't real. It's not a documentary, because all the people in the movie are acting...A social experiment, if you want to call it that.'

When the pair finally announced that it was hoax, Casey said, 'I haven't been able to talk about it for two years, and I wanted people to know this was a planned, staged and scripted work of fiction. I didn't want to have anyone get the wrong idea about Joaquin or anybody else in the film. I wanted people to see the movie for what it really is. My intention was never to fool anybody. There's a big difference between fooling someone and asking them to think. I just wanted people to see the film without any interpretative interference from me or anybody else. I don't know if that was the best way.

'I had never directed a movie. I wasn't sure I could see the whole thing through all by myself. I wanted to know if I could actually run this marathon from beginning to end. Beyond that there were certain ideas that interested me, but I didn't want to make a didactic message movie. There were ideas at play, about the entertainment industry and the media. You can't make a movie about a celebrity without it in some way being about celebrity culture.'

He went on to discuss our obsession with celebrity, how we create them and then destroy them, build them up and then beat them down, and the challenges he faced making the film.

'The challenges just came like waves. It was a challenge to create a story that was interesting; it was a challenge to create performances that were believable, other than from Joaquin, who is so utterly believable, incredibly hard-working, naturally gifted; it was challenging to pull it off technically.

'I was filming it myself and I'd [never done that] and I think it's evident as the movie goes on that it gets better technically, which is how it ought to look: I wanted it that way. It begins as a very innocent, naïve endeavour as one friend makes a movie about another friend. [At the start] it was a tiny, cheap camera, very shaky and grainy. Then, as the story begins to unfold, it starts to look a bit better, until, by the end, it looks technically so much better that it doesn't appear to be a documentary any more.'

And once he'd started, he had to see it through: 'Having something at stake is a great motivator and once this thing became public for me that was very helpful because there was no question: I had to see it through, no matter how long it took. I went broke. I hadn't worked for more than a year, and I was pouring money into the movie. I had to stop for a month to do *The Killer Inside Me*. If I hadn't, I wouldn't have been able to finish the film – I was out of money. There was a lot at stake financially and, if we had left it [the hoax] there, it would have been very damaging to Joaquin's career.'

Joaquin stated, 'Ben Stiller and Sean Combs were both willing to participate without knowing everything about the project. I really appreciated that; I was very moved by people's willingness to be a part of it.

'I'm sure it looked a little bit outrageous, definitely unprofessional. Sometimes it was just me filming it; at most there were only three other people.'

A final word on one of the most talked-about films in 2010 goes to Joaquin, who said simply, 'I wanted to make a movie with my friends and make in a different way. I wanted to have a different experience, and I'm really happy to have done that.'

Joaquin's comeback would still be reported several times, with a number of high-profile roles being linked to him, including that of The Hulk in the superhero movie *The Avengers* and the role of Clyde Tolson in Clint Eastwood's biopic of J. Edgar Hoover. However, Mark Ruffalo ended up landing the role of the green monster, while Eastwood would respond to the rumours in typically gruff manner: 'No. I don't know where that came from. Didn't he become a rapper?'

But with the film a flop and Joaquin out of Hollywood circles for a couple of years he has found himself jumping from golden boy to untouchable with ease. Perhaps that's how he likes it.

Snyder said, 'Take Reese Witherspoon and take Joaquin and look at their career since the film [*Walk the Line*]. I don't know for sure because I haven't worked with Joaquin since 2001 – sometimes actors are their own worst enemy. The difference now is the material.

'We're not England. You guys have great films, and you have independents and stories about people. They're not making them now. Look at the films he's acclaimed for. They're strong character pieces, very strong films. That's the ones we went after.

'Someone like Joaquin, who is an artistic actor, is going to have a hard time finding those kind of scripts in Hollywood.'

It could be a simple case of a man going back to when he enjoyed acting the most, when he had to fight for parts, when there were no expectations and pressure from outside sources.

His *Return to Paradise* director Joseph Ruben stated, 'I kind of suspected it was a role. Joaquin likes to explore strange stuff. A part of him will forget it's an act. This is a guy who will roll down stairs for a laugh. I was kind of worried for him but suspected he was playing a role. Trying something completely different.'

Joaquin once said, 'At the moment, acting is my passion. It's liberating and I love it. Whether that will last, remains to be seen.'

We'll know soon enough if *he's still here*.

JOAQUIN PHOENIX STARS IN THE FILM THAT SHOCKED HOLLYWOOD

"UTTERLY FASCINATING"
VARIETY

"*ENTOURAGE* MEETS *JACKASS!*"
★★★★
LOADED

"THE PERFORMANCE OF HIS LIFETIME"
SUNDAY TIMES CULTURE

OWN IT NOW ON DVD AND